Retail Innovation in Britain:
The Problems of Out-of-Town
Shopping Centre Development

Hugh J. Gayler

Norwich

© H.J. Gayler, 1984.

ISBN 0 86094 154 X

Published by: Geo Books
             Regency House
             Duke Street
             Norwich
             England

Cover illustration:

The photograph on the cover is reproduced
by kind permission of the Hammerson Group

Contents

List of tables

Acknowledgments

This study would not have been possible without the help and encouragement of a number of people. The work was initiated while the author
was on sabbatical leave as a Visiting Lecturer at the University of
Reading, and special thanks must go to Professor Peter Hall, Dr Sophie
Bowlby, Mr John Silk and Dr Erlet Cater of the Department of Geography,
University of Reading, for all the help that was generously given.
Many librarians must be thanked, especially those at Brock University,
the University of Reading and the Department of the Environment; also,
numerous planners and civil servants gave freely of their time to
discuss many of the issues contained within.

I am most grateful to Professor Peter Hall, Dr Sophie Bowlby, Professor
John Jackson (Brock University), Professor Keith Clayton (University
of East Anglia) and an anonymous referee for their comments on an
earlier draft of this text. Thanks also to Joan Gordon, Jenny Gurski,
Irene Richardson and Phyllis Riesberry for struggling with my hand-
writing so successfully.

Last, but not least, my heartfelt appreciations go to my wife, Fran,
for enduring all those absences or being dragged around yet another
shopping centre.

Hugh J. Gayler,
Department of Geography,
Brock University,
St. Catharines, Ontario,
Ontario, Canada, L2S 3A1

August 1983

iv

1. Introduction

In the period since the Second World War there have been
considerable changes in the nature of retailing and consumer
behaviour in Britain. These reflect first of all various
social and economic changes that have affected the population,
including higher disposable incomes, improved levels of
education, greater mobility, increased leisure time and
changing family and employment conditions. Meanwhile, the
role of government in retailing and consumer behaviour has
increased considerably. For better or for worse, shopping
centres are now planned. Both existing and new centres need
planning permission before any construction, major renovation
or even certain changes of use can take place; and massive
public financing has entered into most retail development or
redevelopment schemes. Also, many other government
initiatives, for example road building programmes and
redistribution of population, have indirectly influenced
retailing and consumer behaviour. Finally, the retail
industry itself has been responsible for many changes and
innovations, including the size, number and type of stores,
the nature of ownership and methods of wholesaling and
selling, all of which have been designed, directly or
indirectly, to enhance profitability, reduce costs to the
consumer and give consumers what it is felt they desire.

This study is concerned with one aspect of retail innovation
- the development of the out-of-town shopping centre[1] in
Britain after the mid 1960s. This type of centre can be
defined as one that does not fit either the traditional or
planned retail hierarchy of town centre, district centre(s),
neighbourhood centres and smaller groups of shops; and it is
viewed by government and much of the private sector as

---

[1] Various names may be found for this type of centre, indicating
variations by size, activity and location and the extent to which
terminology by the retail industry, consultants, planners and others
has been adopted. The names given to similar developments outside
Britain are also to be seen. These include edge-of-town centres,
regional centres, suburban and community shopping centres. Frequently,
the centre may be indicated by the nature of the dominant, or sole,
store (e.g. a superstore or hypermarket), or by the name of the firm
(e.g. the Woolco centre or SavaCentre).

undesirable. Most proposals are for out-of-town or at least outer-suburban locations because of land availability, land prices and accessibility for the car-owning consumer; however, there is also, pressure for retail development within older urban areas in various off-centre locations including cleared residential or industrial land and recently developed industrial and warehouse estates. The study will address the wider issue of shopping developments outside the traditional or planned retail hierarchy, as well as the more specific out-of-town location.

The out-of-town shopping centre can hardly be considered a recent innovation influencing consumer behaviour. The first developments in North America began almost fifty years ago, and since then expansion has kept pace with the rise in car ownership, the massive shift of population to lower density, suburban situations, the congested nature and deteriorating physical environment of so many city centre areas and changing demands made by developers, retailers and consumers alike (Jones, 1969). Almost all cities of more than 50 000 people in North America (and also many that are smaller than this) now have one or more shopping centres on their urban fringe, providing an assortment of convenience and shopping goods and competing in many instances with the city centre and the older commercial strips in suburban areas. These shopping centres, depending on the size of the market area, can vary from approximately 200 000 sq.ft. gross floor area (supermarket, discount-department store and smaller chain and specialty stores) to over 2 million sq.ft. (two or more supermarkets, at least two fully-fledged department stores, one or more discount-department stores, two or more cinemas, a variety of fast food establishments and various professional offices, in addition to a wide range of chain and specialty stores).

Meanwhile, in parts of Western Europe, especially France and West Germany, a large number of free-standing superstores have been developed in the last twenty years on the urban fringe (Smith, 1973; Davies, 1979). They vary from expanded supermarkets of 25 000 sq.ft. to vast warehouse-like structures of almost 250 000 sq.ft., and as in the North American case they are surrounded by extensive surface car parking. Traditional supermarket food items, with perhaps specialist bakery, meat, fish and alcohol sections, make up the majority of sales; however, the majority of the floor area may be given over to a wide range of non-food items, including clothing, furniture, appliances, car accessories and garden equipment, in effect resembling a North American discount-department store.

The development of out-of-town shopping centres is just one example of a function, in this case retailing, responding to changing needs in our society. However, many of the problems that arise in urban areas result because the various changes taking place within the one function do not keep up with one another. Some changes are more rapid than others, and eventually the necessary changes that are

2

lagging, or not even taking place, contribute to societal conflicts.

Many urban problems result because changes in technology and human behaviour take place much faster than the changes in the physical structures in the city which accommodate that particular technology and behaviour. Similarly, changes in the attitudes of government, whose support is usually necessary if physical change is to take place, also lag behind. In retailing, changing human behaviour must be partitioned between the receivers of goods and services (the consumer) and those responsible for providing the goods and services (the government through planning and financing, the development industry building shops and shopping centres and the retail organisations and individual retailers selling the goods).

Many changes in the behaviour of consumers are not just related to retailing but affect numerous other functions and activities. One of the most persistent changes leading to retail change in the last forty years has been the suburbanisation of both new and existing urban residents and the establishment of new and expanded urban communities elsewhere (e.g. the British new towns). The result has been an increasing divorce between residential location and the traditional location for the major shopping goods which invariably lies in the city centre. Such a divorce does not bring about a conflict and a desire for retail locational change as long as consumers are content to incur the extra distances that must be travelled. Whether or not consumers do desire a change, the forces of change have been far more responsive in the North American than in the British context. In most North American cities there has been a considerable decline in the proportion of retail space to be found in the centre of the city, reflecting massive suburban developments. But in many cities this suburban development has not led to an absolute decline in retail space in the city core; in the larger cities, especially, office development (and its new daytime population), tourism and conventions and the development of high-order, specialist goods and services have in fact resulted in an increase in retail space.

The second important change in consumer behaviour relates to improved mobility. The last forty years have seen the mass (but by no means universal) ownership of the car in most of the world's leading industrial nations. Consumers are no longer tied to public transportation routes which focus on city centres but are more free to shop in nearby cities and cross-town suburban locations. Two factors aid this shift in preference. First, public authorities have responded to increasing car ownership by building new roads and improving the existing network. However, because of cost, social disruption and public opposition, the most densely populated parts of the inner city have often fallen behind in improvements to their road network. Second, and following from this, consumers find it frustrating and costly to use the car for shopping in the city centre, and as a result many consumers have sought alternate locations for shopping.

A third aspect of change in consumer behaviour results from improvements in standards of living and changes in lifestyle and future expectations. Consumers have a higher level of disposable income which influences the nature and proportions of different products that are purchased. A better educated public is now more demanding, more sophisticated in its tastes, more aware of various facets of retailing and aided by improved mobility has been responsible for keener competition in the industry. A higher proportion of married women in the labour force, as well as other demands made on family time, has resulted in a greater emphasis on convenience, family shopping and the need for weekend and late night shopping. While disposable incomes have increased, more demands are now made on that income with the result that consumers place as much an emphasis as they ever did on attempting to reduce retail costs.

Those concerned with providing the goods and services needed by consumers have traditionally played a twofold role. First of all, from the point of view of business survival, retailers have had to be conscious of consumer needs and change their mode of operation as consumer preferences change. On the other hand, retailers, using new technologies which they believe will lower their costs, improve their competitive position and raise profits, have introduced innovations in their business practices which consumers have often been forced to adopt whether they like them or not. Even where alternatives still exist for the consumer, it is frequently the case that previous practices are more costly, less convenient and may suggest a lower status, and thus there are various advertising and peer group pressures, varying in their subtlety, for consumers to change.

It is often unclear, and the subject of much controversy in many instances, as to whether consumers, as an organised or unorganised group, demand change, or whether the development and retail industry promote change for the supposed benefit of consumers but for the actual benefit of themselves. In the case of changing residential location and transportation mode, the retail industry and public authorities have responded to a need for improving levels of convenience to the consumer. However, an innovation such as self-service was probably never demanded by consumers, but increasingly forced upon them as stores sought to reduce labour costs and remain competitive with other stores which had already done so: the blow to consumers could perhaps be softened, even to the extent of making it look as if consumers desired the change, through the lower prices to be found in self-service operations. It should be noted that many innovations are tested for consumer reaction and modified before they are generally adopted (a situation which might be considered fundamental). But many others may be more speculative since they cannot be pretested: they

4

are introduced and monitored subsequently for consumer reaction. The latter are often changes involving physical structure where one cannot question consumers beforehand about a situation they have not experienced, but once a trial situation has existed similar developments elsewhere can learn from the experience.

The subject of out-of-town shopping centres in Britain is very much caught up in this controversy of whether the consumer, given his or her changing residential location, increased mobility and changing lifestyle is demanding this new, and supposedly improved form of retailing, or whether it is an aggressive development and retail industry which is attempting to mould public authority and consumer attitudes.

The behaviour of consumers and the development and retail industry cannot be separated from the physical structures in which the behaviour is carried out. As their behaviour changes, irrespective of who is responsible, pressure is put on physical structures to change in order to accommodate them. Physical structures refer not only to the shops and shopping centres, but other elements in the urban fabric which are used when shopping or providing retails services, e.g. the road network and car-parking facilities. Invariably any existing physical structure was developed in response to a set of stimuli which may not be found to the same extent today. Retail structure, for example, in the city centre and on suburban arterial roads was developed over a long period in response to consumers who either walked or used public transportation; and until the Second World War those few consumers who had cars could be accommodated with relative ease and little change was necessary. However, since then the rise in car ownership and its use for shopping have been dramatic; but the extent and costs of adapting physical structures to accommodate the car, through improving road access, enhancing circulation, providing more parking facilities and redeveloping property, are so great that these necessary changes are frequently inadequate by the time they are completed. Moreover, stores in inner city areas were built in response to business practices of that day: functional blight and the need to redevelop may result as business practices change.

Accommodating the car and developing stores to suit the needs of today are infinitely easier and cheaper when locating on vacant land in suburban and out-of-town situations. A more realistic ratio of parking spaces to retail floor area (and thus consumer demand) is possible; and shopping centres can be designed to present day specifications, emphasising, for example, the need for larger, one storey buildings for multi -functional operations, much smaller stores for the increasing range of speciality functions, car-pedestrian separation and service access for commercial vehicles. In Britain, however, the vast majority of new shopping projects have been tied either to the existing retail hierarchy or to a newly created or modified retail hierarchy in the case of a new and expanded town developments. The predominant

5

result (in terms of the largest projects) has been the attempt to graft new shopping centre designs and store types on an existing set of city centre streets, rather than follow the North American example of working from the vantage point of a virgin site. Apart from a few new-town centres and district centres in expanding communities, most entirely new and comprehensively planned shopping centres in Britain are little more than a redesign of traditional neighbourhood and community shopping facilities, emphasising an off-street, as opposed to an on-street location.

The development of out-of-town centres in Britain is an intrusion which upsets the existing or planned retail hierarchy. They are like suburban shopping centres in North America in that they compete with one or more city centre areas: the degree of competition depends on the size of both the city centre and the out-of-town centre and the extent to which the city-region may be growing, and whether or not the city is growing these centres upset the traditional structure at the neighbourhood and community level.

The issue of out-of-town shopping centres in Britain is one that has sparked much controversy between the various interested parties. On the one hand there has been a fairly aggressive development and retail industry, albeit a very small part of it, which has been able to bring about some change through local government acquiescence and some professional support. But for the most part the industry has faced both opposition from local and central government politicians and civil servants, local chambers of commerce, professional groups and concerned citizens, and indifference on the part of consumers and other sectors of the retail industry. The strength of the forces of conservation and protectionism has resulted in a small and haphazard development of out-of-town superstores and hypermarkets, but more important, an increasing degree of compromise between the two sides whereby superstores have been incorporated into the retail hierarchy in town and district centres. With one notable exception, and even this can scarcely be regarded as out-of-town, there has been a complete shut-out of the American-style, large, regional shopping centre.

This issue is more than simply a battle of wills between two different groups. It is a multi-faceted problem and there is a need to look at the various important factors that are involved. In Chapter 2 it will be seen that the development of out-of-town shopping centres is a logical sequence in a changing retail scene, and it is necessary to look at the forces that have brought about change. Since the Second World War the tremendous decline in the number of retail establishments and changes in their administrative organisation, type and size have affected their spatial organisation in terms of both the inter- and intra-urban retail hierarchy. Chapter 3 will focus on the impact, or likely impact, of out-of-town shopping centres and the nature of consumer preference for this type of activity. Much of

6

the opposition to these centres is based on very wild and inaccurate claims of the damage they will cause, and there is little reference to the many impact studies that have been carried out in the last ten years. The development of out-of-town shopping centres has brought up a number of land use planning problems and conflicts on the rural-urban fringe. Chapter 4 will examine the issues such as urban encroachment and the protection of the countryside, traffic hazards and the intrusive nature of many of the site characteristics of such shopping centres. Many objections to development have been based on the undesirable aspects of physical change. The success, or lack of success, of out-of-town shopping centres has in part been the result of public attitudes towards them, attitudes which reflect fears (real or imagined) and propaganda (both for and against). Chapter 5 will look at the resistance to retail change from the point of view of the various groups involved, the way in which the planning process can be used to oppose change and the nature of that resistance. Chapter 6 will then examine how the workings of government policy have enabled that resistance to be so effective.

Retailing and consumer behaviour are very much on-going processes, and the issues facing the public and private sectors today are very different in many instances from ten years ago. Many of the wider economic and social forces that influence the retail scene are changing, and therefore one is seeing different responses on the part of the various interested parties. On the other hand, the climate of conservatism, protectionism and fear of innovation goes on, resulting in so much change being *ad hoc*, inconsistent and spatially uneven, not comprehensively planned and likely to create future problems. By way of conclusion Chapter 7 will review current issues concerning out-of-town shopping centres and will attempt to forecast likely outcomes into the next decade.

2. Changing retail structure

For many years now the existing retail structure in Britain has been undergoing change from the point of view of numbers of shops, their organization, functions and locational requirements (Scott, 1970; Davies, 1976; Dawson, 1980; Guy, 1980), and it is important to consider the out-of-town shopping centre in the context of overall retail change. It is all too often believed that the out-of-town shopping centre is the sole, major change in retail structure. This is because it is highly visible and controversial; it has attracted the attention of so many people in recent years (academics, government, industry and groups and individuals in favour or opposed to the idea) and has been the subject of discussion from learned journals to the popular press. Other changing elements in the retail structure are just as fundamental and often have caused more problems, but they are able to maintain a much lower profile and have not generated the same amount of debate. The out-of-town shopping centre problem is not simply one of locational change. Underlying this change are issues concerning the nature of the retail industry, in terms of numbers and organization, the differing needs of the various types of out-of-town centres and the relationship between out-of-town centres and existing centres in both an inter-urban and intra-urban context.

2.1 RETAIL DECLINE

A feature of retailing since the Second World War has been the 40 per cent decline in the total number of shops over a thirty year period (Table 2.1). This decline has affected all but one of the retail categories, varying from an enormous 60 per cent in food to 11 per cent in household goods. Only the larger, multi-functional operations have shown an increase. Also, decline has been uneven over time with change in the 1970s contrasting very sharply with that in the 1950s.

These changes reflect various forces ar work in the economic and social life of the country. First of all, certain changes in retail organization and enlarging the space in which the operation is carried out allow for economies of

8

Table 2.1.   Changes in the number of retail establishments in the
             United Kingdom, 1950-80

Retail establishments	1950	1961	1971	1980	% change
Food	283 576	278 458	197 807	118 083	- 58.4
Confectioners, tobacconists/ newsagents	74 606	70 662	52 064	54 878	- 26.4
Clothing/footwear	97 162	96 612	81 279	57 069	- 41.3
Household goods	65 795	69 133	70 342	58 267	- 11.4
Other non-food	60 392	58 692	66 724	50 783	- 15.9
General stores (Dept. variety)	1 641	3 750	4 775	9 520	+480.1
TOTAL	583 132	577 307	472 991	348 601	- 40.1

Source: Board of Trade, 1964. *Report on the census of dis-
        tribution and other services.* 1961, (H.M.S.O., Lon-
        don); Department of Industry, 1975. *Report on the
        census of distribution and other retailing services,
        1971.* (H.M.S.O., London); Department of Industry,
        1980. *Business monitor: retailing.* Business Statis-
        tics office, SDA 25, (H.S.M.O., London).

scale which can be passed on the consumer in the form of
lower prices (National Economic Development Office, 1971).
In the food trades the decline in the number of shops
reflects the rise of the supermarket with its emphasis on
an ever increasing sales area, self-service operation, the
integration of many former specialist goods (e.g. bakery and
greengrocery items) and its expansion into other everyday
household requirements (e.g. small electrical and hardware
items). The out-of-town shopping centre, especially those
consisting of a single superstore or hypermarket, must be
viewed as a logical extension of the supermarket idea, rather
than some revolutionary new trend in retailing.

Second, the decline in the number of shops in Britain
reflected an overprovision of shops in many parts of the
country. Pollard and Hughes (1955) noted that the older
industrial towns contained shops that were below the
national average in terms of size. There were simply too
many corner stores liberally spread through the older and
poorer residential areas and long ribbons of shops along the
major arterial roads through these same areas. Improvements
in living standards, for example the declining need to
depend on a local grocery store for credit, and subsequent
changes in consumer preference have led to the demise of
much local shopping.

The actual eradication of shops may await two further developments. One is the retirement of the retailer. The decline of many small, marginal, one shop businesses can be associated with the retailer finding better means of employment or the ageing of the retailer and the decreasing ability and desire to be competitive, especially if there is no obvious person to carry on the business after retirement. With retirement the shop may change retail function, or where ownership and rents permit it may become a residence.

A second development which has reduced the overprovision of shops is urban renewal. Many of the corner stores and long parades of small shops were found in the older inner city areas where much of the housing was substandard and the areas lacked accepted urban amenities. Moreover, the population of most of these areas had severely declined and the market potential for local shops had decreased. Urban renewal was seen as a way of removing both physical and economic blight and providing the smaller rehoused population with better facilities. However, urban renewal has frequently not taken account of consumer needs, and what may have been an overprovision of shops can become an underprovision as local planning authorities restrict the numbers and location of shops.[1] The result is an increasing dependence by the inner city residents on larger shops, especially in the central area, and bus travel as opposed to walking. Furthermore, Berry, Parsons and Platt (1968) have shown that the relocation process itself can have a serious effect on even prosperous small shops; factors of importance include disruption caused by a temporary cessation of trade, the temporary or permanent loss of customers and the need to pay higher rents if relocating in the new development.

The decline in the number of retail facilities also reflects major shifts of residential population which have taken place in the last forty years. Virtually all of Britain's major cities have declined in population; and if not, they, together with the smaller towns, have experienced decline in their inner areas (through urban renewal and an ageing population) which has been more than made up by suburban expansion (Hall, Gracey, Drewett and Thomas, 1973). However, a major failing of the British planning system is possibly that the decentralization of population to suburban areas and beyond has not been accompanied by the decentralization of the many activities on which people depend, especially employment and retail services. The decline of shops in the inner city through population loss has not been made up by the development of new outlets in outer areas. Unless the new residential development either takes place in an adjacent community with an already established commercial core and a wide

---

[1] This is a problem which is currently being addressed, in association with numerous studies on the British inner city (Moir, 1981; National Economic Development Office, 1981).

range of retail services, or is very large, it is likely that retail services will be limited to the neighbourhood type and residents will still be expected to patronise the city centre for non-convenience items. Local planning authorities play an important role in influencing the level of retailing in both private and public residential developments. They control the number of shops (providing for a fairly standardised grouping of shops in ratio to a certain population) and their location. Not only is the number of shops limited, but their location in small centres, together with a lower density of population, contributes to worse levels of accessibility compared to the traditional inner city pattern (Guy, 1976; 1980).

The trend to larger stores has resulted in a decline in the number of retail establishments in all but one of the durable goods categories (Table 2.1). However, this decline is not as severe as in the food category, and is a reflection of rising living standards and the greater amount of disposable income that is available for spending on luxury items such as furniture and household appliances. A trend associated with this is the increasing number of speciality stores providing services which were hitherto contained within more general stores, e.g. greeting cards, bathroom accessories and leather goods.

2.2 RETAIL ORGANISATION

The trend to fewer and larger retail establishments has in part been aided by organizational shifts in the industry itself. From the point of view of the British census retail establishments are classified on the basis of independents (individuals or firms operating fewer than ten outlets), multiples (individuals or firms operating ten or more outlets) and co-operatives (stores operated by the many co-operative societies). Table 2.2 shows that in the period 1950-80 the number of independent stores has decreased by nearly one half and the number of co-operative stores by almost two thirds, although in terms of the proportion of stores operated by the three groups the change has been much smaller and the independents still have a very strong hold in numerical terms. However, the number of stores gives no indication as to their size and the income that can be generated. Table 2.3 shows that proportional shifts of turnover have been more traumatic. Both co-operatives and independents have lost ground in favour of the multiples.

The increasing share of the market controlled by multiple organisations is indicative of their ability to compete more favourably than independent stores. Factors such as central control, centralised buying and the large turnover of any multiple organisation result in economies of scale which are not available for most independent retailers. Second, multiple organisations have sufficient capital to invest in various forms of product, market, store and site research, the outcome of which gives them even greater competitive edge over independent retailers. Third, multiple organisations

Table 2.2. Changes in the number of retail establishments in the U.K. by organisation, 1950-1980.

Retail Establishment	1950	%	1961	%	1971	%	1980	%
Co-ops	25 544	4.4	29 396	5.1	15 413	3.2	8 556	2.5
Multiples	53 949	9.2	67 299	11.7	66 785	14.1	65 241	18.7
Independents	503 639	86.4	480 612	83.2	390 793	82.7	274 804	78.8
TOTAL	583 132	100.0	577 307	100.0	472 991	100.0	348 601	100.0

Source: Board of Trade, 1964. *Report on the census of distribution and other services. 1961,* (H.M.S.O., London); Department of Industry, 1975. *Report on the census of distribution and other services, 1971.* (H.M.S.O., London); Department of Industry, 1980. *Business monitor: retailing.* Business Statistics Office, SDA 25, (H.M.S.O., London).

Table 2.3. Changes in the turnover of retail establishments in the U.K. by organisation, 1950-1980.

Retail Establishment	1950 £000m	%	1961 £000m	%	1971 £000m	%	1980 £000m	%
Co-ops	572	11.4	959	10.8	1 108	7.1	3 869	6.6
Multiples	1 093	21.9	2 580	28.9	6 083	39.0	28 046	48.0
Independents	3 335	66.7	5 379	60.3	8 419	53.9	26 569	45.4
TOTAL	5 000	100.0	8 918	100.0	15 610	100.0	58 484	100.0

Source: Board of Trade, 1964. *Report on the census of distribution and other services. 1961,* (H.M.S.O., London); Department of Industry, 1975. *Report on the census of distribution and other services, 1971.* (H.M.S.O., London); Department of Industry, 1980. *Business monitor: retailing.* Business Statistics Office, SDA 25, (H.M.S.O., London).

have the added advantage of being better able to afford the
higher rents to be in the best locations (i.e. the highly
travelled sections of a city centre). Fourth, once
government legislation abolished resale price maintenance
in 1964, multiple organisations were better able to cut
prices and attract custom.

It is interesting to compare government sponsored research,
reviewing likely developments in the retail trades, to what
actually happened. It was suggested that the number of
stores would decline to approximately 400 000 by 1980
(National Economic Development Office, 1971). Moreover,
multiple organisations would increase their share of the
total market at the expense of independent retailers. At
the same time the trend to fewer and larger stores would
continue amongst the multiple organisations as rationalisation
took place through takeovers and or marginal locations,
duplication and overlapping hinterlands being eliminated.
It would seem that predictions held true, although the
severity of the decline in the total number of establishments
was underestimated (Tables 2.1-2.3).

Depending on the number of stores operated, co-operative
societies can be considered as independents or multiples.
But for statistical purposes they are treated separately,
largely because of their different organisation: the public
can be members of an individual society, can play a role in
running it and in the past could receive dividends based on
the value of purchases made. In spite of rationalisation,
including the takeover of small societies and the removal of
small stores in the declining inner city, the co-operative
societies have languished and now have a mere 6.6 per cent
of the retail trade (Table 2.3). Earlier, it had been
expected that trade would stabilise as co-operative societies
adopted the same aggressive trading practices as multiple
organisations. For example, some societies began operating
superstores (Thomas, Thorpe and McGoldrick, 1977). However,
attempts to copy multiple organisations and improve their
trading position have been far from universal. Co-operative
society development may be hampered by the image that they
still present. Their importance amongst a working class
population still persists. Various surveys (e.g. Sunderland
Corporation, 1971) have shown that Co-op stores receive a
disproportionate share of customers in the D and E social
groups (semi-skilled and unskilled blue-collar occupations,
the unemployed and the retired). Moreover in keeping with
the greater popularity of Co-op stores before the 1950s,
they still receive a disproportionate share of customers in
the over 45 age group. As long as most co-operative societies
shun large superstore and hypermarket operations, there is
little likelihood of breaking out of this mould and improving
their trading position.

13

2.3 MULTIPLES AND THE SUPERMARKET-SUPERSTORE

In many respects the growth of one of the types of out-of-town shopping centre, that focussing on a superstore or hypermarket, is associated with the development of supermarkets by multiple organisations, their increasing size and the need for improved locations. The move towards supermarkets began in Britain in the 1950s as multiple organisations and co-operatives converted their existing operations; but increasingly as the retail industry and public authorities became interested in redevelopment in the town centre, larger supermarkets were incorporated into the design and were purpose built.

By 1970, and before the onset of superstore development, there were some 28 000 supermarkets in Britain compared to almost 200 000 grocery and other food stores, but these supermarkets received 70 per cent of the grocery trade and 35 per cent of all food trade (Institute of Food Distribution, 1970). Their impact has been considerable: four years before that there were 22 000 supermarkets, compared to 227 000 grocery and other food stores, receiving 57 per cent of the grocery trade and 24 per cent of all food trade.

The various census reports relating to retailing indicate that in the food trade it is the largest multiple organisations that have received an increasing share of total sales. Table 2.4 shows that the independents and the smallest multiple organisations (10-19 shops) have suffered a relative decline in turnover. Meanwhile, the greatest impact on food sales has been made by the national supermarket chains which each have more than a 100 stores. Over the last thirty years their hold on food sales has gone from a relatively unimportant 17 per cent to over 40 per cent, and now outstrips that of the independent retailer. The developments by supermarket chains with strong regional affinities, as well as the rationalisation carried out by national chains, have resulted in an impressive increase in the food trade in the 50-99 shops category. It may be argued that the decline in the proportion of trade by independent retailers would have been more catastrophic had it not been for the voluntary association of retailers with wholesalers and thus the opportunity to reduce prices through bulk purchasing (Cohen, 1961).

For the most part the development of supermarkets in the 1960s by the largest multiple organisations could be termed the 'Battle of the High Street Giants', since the largest supermarkets were principally located in the town centres and many associated with comprehensive development schemes. However, increasingly, this type of location has presented problems to both retailer and consumer alike. First, many of the supermarket schemes were conceived at a time when a smaller proportion of the population owned cars. Frequently, no parking was provided close to the store, or it was inadequate in terms of the amount and its location. With the trend towards once-a-week bulk purchasing the need to use a car to transport the goods home becomes more essential. The scenario,

Table 2.4

Changes in the turnover of food stores in
the United Kingdom, 1950-80

Retailers having	1950 £000 millions	%	1961 £000 millions	%	1971 £000 millions	%	1980 £000 millions	%
less than 10 shops (independents)	631	71.1	1 083	63.2	1 765	48.9	7 772	34.4
10-19 shops	33	3.7	53	3.2	102	2.8 }	1 957	8.7
20-49 shops	33	3.7	83	4.8	263	7.3 }		
50-99 shops	35	4.0	51	3.0	132	3.7	3 233	14.3
more than 100 shops	155	17.5	440	25.8	1 344	37.4	9 624	42.6
TOTAL	887	100.0	1 710	100.0	3 606	100.0	22 586	100.0

Source: Board of Trade, 1964. *Report on the census of distribution and other services. 1961,* (H.M.S.O., London); Department of Industry, 1975. *Report on the census of distribution and other services, 1971.* (H.M.S.O., London); Department of Industry, 1980. *Business monitor: retailing.* Business Statistics Office, SDA 25, (H.M.S.O., London).

which is all too common in British town centres today, is
that the necessary multi-storey car parking is not
conveniently situated or is poorly designed. For example,
it is found to be on the periphery of the central area and
associated with an inner ring road system rather than a
supermarket. Lifts in the car park frequently will not take
shopping carts, or there are stairs instead of a lift. On
the other hand, where parking is convenient to the
supermarket, there may be problems of road access, especially
at peak shopping times. For example, a queue of cars waiting
to get into a car park can clog a city street; or, in order
to beat the queue getting out, drivers will park, even double
park, in the street outside the supermarket waiting for their
passengers and their groceries. There is consequently a loss
of shopping amenity and a desire by retailers and consumers
alike for more convenient shopping locations. The incidence
of town centre traffic congestion is sufficient to warrant
the central government's attention, but the response has been
to encourage the district centre in a town's suburbs for
relocating central-area convenience goods rather than the
out-of-town centre (Ministry of Housing and Local Government,
1969).

A second problem concerns the movement of goods on the part
of the commercial vehicle (Pain, 1967). Access to stores
for lorries is especially difficult in many of Britain's
oldest cities, and often not well planned for in redevelopmen
schemes (for example, the lack of underground or off-street
loading facilities). The all too familiar scene is one of
lorries loading or off-loading at the kerbside contributing
to further congestion. Pain (1967) noted that there was
little understanding on the part of local authorities of the
commercial vehicle problem. It would perhaps be fair to say
that understanding is better today, but there may be an
inability to do anything about the problem, short of closing
the store; although the removal of the private car on many
central area streets has certainly eased the situation.

Third, the inappropriateness of the town centre for
supermarket shopping has been associated with developments
in the mid 1960s in the industry itself. At this time there
was an increasing number of plans, and planning permissions,
for ever larger supermarkets, commonly called superstores and
hypermarkets (Guy, 1980).[1] This was a development that was
already underway in Western Europe although it should be note
that, unlike the British case, there was no slow transition

---

[1] In the British context there is no official definition of what
constitutes a superstore or hypermarket. A definition by the Unit for
Retail Planning Information (1976), which has been adopted as a rule of
thumb by the retail industry and government, states that superstores have
a minimum of 25 000 sq.ft. of selling space and hypermarkets a minimum of
50 000 sq.ft. of selling space; both are accompanied by car parking,
operate on a single floor, are self-service and offer food and non-food
items.

from small independent food stores to larger and larger
multiple-owned supermarkets (Smith, 1973; Thorncroft, 1973;
Davies, 1979); instead there was a rapid move to superstores
and hypermarkets and a change of location to suburban and
out-of-town situations. Compared to British High Street
supermarkets of the 1960s, varying from 4 000 to 10 000 sq.
ft. of selling space, continental superstores were mostly
built with between 25 000 and 100 000 sq.ft. of selling
space as free-standing structures surrounded by acres of
surface car parking, similar in many respects to the American
regional shopping centre. Also, there was no longer a
dependence on selling food items; as much as 75 per cent of
the selling area and 40 per cent of sales may be devoted to
non-convenience items, including clothing, hardware, electrical
goods, gardening items, car service and restaurant facilities.

The largest British multiple organisations, together with
some co-operative societies and French hypermarket interests,
viewed continental superstores and hypermarkets as a means
whereby they could introduce further economies of scale,
better compete with respect to their rivals in the supermarket
business and hopefully improve their service to the customer.
However, the industry did not always consider the traditional
High Street location, or even the district centre, as
appropriate for larger forms of supermarket, or superstores[1]
(Kivell, 1972). Land building costs were considered to be
too great in the town centre, especially if the selling area
was to be on the one level, and given the size of area
required there were doubts as to land availability. Moreover,
virtually all planning authorities now require car parking
provision based on the square footage of retail space; and
new developments in the town centre must be accompanied by,
or related to, local car parking capacity, whether financed
by the public or private sector. Again, costs were
considered by operators to be too high when compared to
alternative locations. There was also the fact that there
might already be sufficient supermarket provision in the town
centre, and any new space would need to attract consumers
away from other shopping locations: planning authorities
increasingly thought it desirable to consider these other
locations.

---

[1]There has been resistance by most multiple organisations to the use of
the word hypermarket because of its connotation with large-scale
development in strictly out-of-town locations, thereby upsetting other
retailers, politicians, planners and the general public. The word
superstore is meant to soften the blows, even cloud the issue, helped
by the fact that many developments are small and can be incorporated
into town and district centre schemes. Indeed, customer and government
acceptance is now such that stores with less than 25 000 sq.ft. of
selling space are 'cashing in' and being called superstores (Institute
of Grocery Distribution, 1982; Jones, P.M., 1982).

The trend towards the development of superstores in Britain by the retail industry has been distinctly in favour of non-central locations. But at the same time the locations that have been approved vary considerably in their type. It is difficult to obtain precise figures on how many superstores there are, since development has been large and rapid and the count varies according to which organisation is doing it. According to the Unit for Retail Planning Information (Jones, P.M., 1982) some 230 stores over 25 000 sq.ft. of selling space (188 superstores and 42 hypermarkets) were open at the end of 1981, compared to 100 in 1976 and 3 in 1967. Only a handful of these are in free-standing, out-of-town (or even in-town) locations, and therefore not part of the traditional or planned, retail hierarchy; while their numbers may be small, their size and location and the controversy this has generated have resulted in considerable publicity and research, and this will be examined below. The bulk of superstore development has gone ahead unobtrusively because it has fitted in with local authority plans and has not raised the ire of other business interests, central government or the general public. The bulk of superstores are to be found in existing town and city centres, planned new-town centres (for example, the Carrefour hypermarket in Telford), planned district centres in new and expanded town schemes (for example, Weston Favell in Northampton) and other new or existing district centres (for example, the Asda superstore in Lower Earley, Reading).

The total number of superstores and hypermarkets in Britain is fast approaching the French or West German situation, although in the continental European case most stores are in true out-of-town locations. The lag in the British situation is partly the continuing love-affair with the High Street supermarket and its expansion into the central area shopping precinct superstore; and any move away from town centres has been to district centres. Superstore organisations have all too often fallen into line with government thinking in order to have their schemes approved. To hold out for an out-of-town location approval is to invite years of frustration, delay, high legal costs and most likely a refusal anyway.

2.4 THE DEVELOPMENT OF THE REGIONAL SHOPPING CENTRE

The second type of out-of-town shopping centre, after the superstore or hypermarket, is the planned regional shopping centre, a development originating in North America rather than continental Europe. This is a purpose-built, free-standing structure consisting of a one or more department stores, discount-department stores, a variety of other convenience and shopping goods stores, and some non-retail activities, contained in an open or enclosed mall and surrounded by surface car parking facilities (Sternlieb and Hughes, 1981).[1] Unlike the superstore the emphasis in such

---

[1] In the North American context planned shopping centres selling a majority of comparison or shopping goods are distinguished according to size and thus the population threshold needed for their support (Berry, 1963). The smaller centres, up to approximately 400 000 sq.ft. gross floorspace, are termed community shopping centres, whilst those over that figure are regional centres.

a centre is on shopping rather than convenience goods (and
thus in competition with one or more city centre areas),
and compared to a superstore of equivalent size it needs a
more extensive hinterland to support it.

There is only one large regional shopping centre in Britain,
the 790 000 sq.ft. (gross floor space) Brent Cross shopping
centre in north west London which was opened in March 1976.
However, there are a number of smaller centres, not exceeding
150 000 sq.ft. which focus on a Woolco (F.W. Woolworth)
discount department store, in addition to as many as fifteen
smaller units leased by the development company to independent
retailers and multiple organisations (Thorpe and Kivell,1971;
Thorpe *et al.*, 1972). Unlike their operations in North America
the Woolco stores contain a supermarket which constitutes up
to 30 per cent of the store's total sales. However, because
of the small size of these regional centres and their
dominace by one store, they are invariably included under the
same heading as superstores.

The uniqueness of Brent Cross, as well as its commanding
presence, enormous impact and the potential damage if copied,
have resulted in it receiving considerable attention by
government, business and academics (Department of the
Environment, 1970; Black, 1976; Lee and Kent, 1977; Shepherd
and Newby, 1978; Newby and Shepherd, 1979). This centre is
located on the North Circular Road, close to the A5, A41 and
M1 roads and to the Northern Line of the London Underground,
and the enclosed retail space on two levels includes two major
department stores, and a hundred other stores, most of them
multiples. The forty acre site contains some 4 500 surface
and multi-storey car parking spaces, and the importance of
car borne shopping has resulted in a network of access roads
to connect the shopping centre with surrounding main roads.
While Brent Cross is a free-standing regional shopping centre,
developed and built by the private sector, it can hardly be
regarded as out-of-town. It was built in an area of Greater
London which was principally developed before the Second
World War and is now experiencing a population decline. One
of the developer's major arguments was that the shopping
centre would bring a quality of shopping facilities which was
currently absent in the north west London area; consumers
had to travel to Central London (the West End) in order to
find something similar. As a result, Brent Cross received
some acceptance by government, and in the Greater London
Development Plan it featured as one of the eight major
strategic centres in London's suburbs. However, the proposal
generated considerable controversy and it was almost fifteen
years between the initial planning and actual opening.

The experiences of other potential regional shopping centre
developers has not encouraged a flood of applications to
build North American style out-of-town centres. The opposition
and inherent protectionist attitudes of local authorities,
together with the strengths of the existing retail hierarchy,
have not made it a favourable climate in which to invest
and seek a return on capital. Only five other regional
shopping centre proposals have reached the planning approval

stage and all were refused. The first was at Haydock Park, Lancashire in 1964 and was the subject of detailed research that has acted as a benchmark by which to judge subsequent out-of-town shopping centre applications (University of Manchester, Department of Town and Country Planning, 1964). The proposal called for building a centre of approximately one million sq.ft.; since the area was not expanding rapidly in population terms, it was suggested that in order for the centre to be successful it would have to jeopardise the commercial viability of existing centres (Department of the Environment, 1965[1]). The effects that out-of-town centres would have on existing centres were major reasons for rejecting the other four applications: Wolvercote, Oxford (Department of the Environment, 1972a); Cribbs Causeway, bear Bristol (Department of the Environment, 1974); Stonebridge, Solihull (Department of the Environment, 1975a); and Roselands, Broxstowe, Nottinghamshire (Department of the Environment 1975b).

The wider issues of competition between new and existing centres will be pursued in more detail in Chapters 5 and 6. From the point of view of changing retail structure, the establishment of large, shopping goods centres and also superstores in other than town and district centres can be viewed as alien to tradition, since these centres upset the status quo arrangement of shopping centres in both the inter-urban and intra-urban context. It is only natural that a comment such as this should frequently be made by certain vested interests, both public and private, which stand to gain by protecting the status quo. However, the more impartial observer has also questioned the effects of introducing a new type of retail centre. There is a fear that the British town centre will take on the appearance of so many North American city centres (without realising that it is not just retail change that has led to the deteriorating situation in some North American city centres). Moreover, it is felt that free-standing out-of-town shopping centres are primarily for private financial gain whereas the existing retail structure identifies with the wider community interest and acts as a focal point for various community interactions; weakening this retail structure may seriously affect other social and economic activities.

Compared to the existing retail hierarchy, seen in 2.5 and 2.6 below, the out-of-town shopping centre, be it a regional shopping centre or a superstore, is heavily geared to the car owning shopper. At Brent Cross, for example, 75 per cent of shopping trips are made by car (at some out-of-town superstores the figure can be as high as 90 per cent), compared to 21 per cent of all British shopping trips (Shepherd and Newby, 1978)

---

[1] At the time of the government's decision the file on the planning application was held by the Ministry of Housing and Local Government. That Ministry was absorbed into the Department of the Environment in June, 1970. All file numbers and dates are given under the Department of the Environment.

The difference in the figures reflects the fact that Brent Cross is not an important local shopping centre (therby encouraging a high proportion of journeys on foot) but attracts consumers over a wide area of both the inner and outer north west London suburbs and the Home Counties beyond, aided no doubt by improved road communications affecting time-distance relationships. Furthermore, the up-market nature of shopping at Brent Cross appeals to a consumer group where car ownership is far higher than the national average. Undoubtedly, proposals for out-of-town centres are aimed at exploiting the various benefits to the car-owning shopper. On the other hand, the traditional retail hierarchy is associated with a far higher proportion of journeys on foot to local neighbourhood and district centres and of bus journeys to the central area of the city.

2.5 THE INTER-URBAN RETAIL HIERARCHY

The growth of out-of-town shopping centres can have serious implications for the existing retail structure. Just how serious will obviously depend on the number of new centres, their size, their location with respect to existing facilities and the extent to which the intended hinterland of the new centre is expanding in population and thus justifying more retail space. However, whether or not an area population is expanding, new forms of retailing put pressure on existing facilities. Out-of-town superstores emphasise factors such as discount operations and economies of scale which can result in price undercutting of existing stores; second, as outlined in 2.1 above, existing operations may be physically inadequate in many ways since they were built for a different set of conditions, while new developments heighten these inadequacies and encourage changes in patronage.

The distribution of retail facilities has been related to the central place theory concepts of range and threshold. These are concepts which denote respectively the distance a person is prepared to travel in order to purchase a good and the minimum purchasing power necessary to support a good in a particular central place (Berry and Garrison, 1958a; 1958b). The result is a hierarchial spatial structure of central places. Those functions with the smallest thresholds will enter the central place hierarchy on the lowest level. In any area these lowest-order centres will be the most numerous, and thus have the shortest distance between them. Moreover, they will carry the smallest total number of functions. Successive higher-order centres in the hierarchy will not only include new goods with larger thresholds but also the goods found in lower-order centres. Thus, with each higher-order centre there will be an increase in the total number of functions and the distance between similar centres and a decrease in their frequency of occurrence.

In an inter-urban context the position of a particular town in the central place hierarchy is determined first by the size of that town (Thorpe, 1968). This reflects the threshold available within an acceptable range; moreover, these consumers can be regarded as a captive audience since similar retail facilities in any other town are naturally further away. A second factor is the size and nature of the total market area, including the number and location of lower-order towns and the socio-economic standing of the market area population. Davies (1968), for example, points out that the second factor is more important than the first, and in Carruther's (1967) classification of shopping centres in England and Wales it can be seen that towns with similar populations are different in terms of their total retail sales and the provision of various retail facilities.

The hierarchy of shopping centres is not something that is static; changes in the relative standings of the various towns reflect a number of factors including changes in retail organisation, redevelopment schemes, population change and improved mobility. Examination of the various census reports would indicate that the major centres (e.g. Birmingham, Manchester and Leeds) have not changed in importance; but many inner metropolitan centres and centres in the older, slow-growth industrial town have declined in relative importance, while outer metropolitan centres and faster expanding towns in the Midlands and south east England have increased (Smith, 1968).

The large out-of-town comparison goods centre should be viewed dispassionately as a form of retail organisation, yet it is also an element in the retail hierarchy which is going to influence the relative importance of surrounding centres. This is no different from the competition that has been taking place for some considerable time between many of Britain's historic towns or as a result of the intrusion of a new or expanded town shopping centre. However, the large out-of-town centre is viewed with anything but dispassion. The competition between existing centres or with a new-town shopping centre has the stamp of central government approval and is played at the local level with all the elements of fair play, blessed by the political structures in the various towns who frequently meet one another in various social situations. The initiatives of one town in urban renewal and expanding or replacing retail space are rarely opposed by another town; they merely create a need for the other town to devise or speed up its initiatives in this area. On the other hand, out-of-town centres are a new form of development that do not fit into the existing order. They are promoted by outside property development companies and the national multiple organisations who will lease the stores, and there is little or no allegiance attempted with the local business and political community. Any proposal to build an out-of-town centre is immediately seen as a threat to the existing order in one or more towns, and since the local politician holds the key to planning approval at the local level it is easy for the out-of-town centre to be rejected.

The fears of the political and business community concerning the effects of large out-of-town centres on the inter-urban retail hierarchy is supported by the research carried out on the Haydock Park proposal (University of Manchester, Department of Town and Country Planning, 1964). It was suggested that

22

by 1971 Liverpool, Manchester and Bolton could lose as much as 12 per cent of their total sales, while for Preston and Crewe it could be 16 per cent, and for towns closer to Haydock Park the losses were St. Helens (34 per cent), Wigan (41 per cent) and Warrington (46 per cent). Various redevelopment projects and proposals in these towns would be financially handicapped, and the whole commercial viability of Skelmersdale New Town could be undermined.

However, the repercussions from any one town expanding its retail facilities can be equally serious. In the inter-urban context the use of predictive models in the planning of retail facilities has been widespread (National Economic Development Office, 1970; Jackson, 1972). But often the variables most commonly included, such as population, measures of the retail facilities themselves and distance that consumers travel, are not always the most sound; in ten or twenty years hence the behaviour of consumers, retail organisations and government could have changed drastically, and there may have been a substantial overprediction of changes in population and retail sales. The result is that there has tended to be more short term planning considerations, carried on at a more local level and attempting to take into account various current trends in shopping.[1] But given the fragmentary nature of local government and the lack of incentive to co-ordinate their efforts, there has been in many instances an overprovision of retail space (Mills, 1974). It is not that the methods used to estimate future shopping space were so radically wrong, but that two or more towns could not readily define their hinterland boundaries; thus, they tended to be too generous to themselves, and consequently a proportion of the population was supposed to shop regularly in more than one town.

The overprovision of retail space by any one town can be seen in the high vacancy rates of both old and new properties or the underutilisation of space; this presents to the town a loss of rateable income and a lack of return on any public monies invested, and vacant property gives an air of insecurity and perhaps a blighted appearance which may deter shoppers. The overprovision is often deliberate. First, it can be an attempt by private and public interests (which subsequently failed) to increase retail sales at the expense of one or more adjacent towns: of course to succeed, and have no overprovision of space, may create an overprovision of space elsewhere. Second, multiple organisations look upon new and improved retail space as a way of increasing their share of the market over other multiples and independent retailers, which local authorities publicly condone because of the financial returns involved. The result may be a high vacancy rate in older

---

[1] It should be noted that local authorities can be highly selective in the current trends they wish to emphasise. They may, for example, note that consumers are using their cars more for shopping and subsequently provide more multi-storey parking in the town centre, but not see that they may prefer to use their cars to shop in out-of-town or district centre locations.

properties which encourages demolition, conversion or further efforts to attract retailers, all of which reduce the over-provision of space. However, until such property adjustments are made, there can be an unattractive shopping environment.

Clearly, large out-of-town shopping centres should not be opposed simply because they may influence the economic viability of the existing inter-urban retail hierarchy. That hierarchy is neither static nor sacrosanct but has been undergoing change for some time. The introduction of out-of-town centres would merely result in further readjustments which need not be any more detrimental than those taking place at present. The readjustments would substantially improve the shopping environment, for example taking the pressure off existing facilities and relieving traffic congestion in many town centres (University of Manchester, Department of Town and Country Planning, 1964; Ministry of Housing and Local Government, 1969).

The smaller out-of-town shopping centres, constituting super-stores and concentrating on convenience goods, especially food can also have an impact on the inter-urban retail hierarchy. Superstores on the edge of, for example, Carruther's (1967) third-order towns or centres can effect the viability of nearby fourth-order or even smaller centres, especially since these centres have a higher proportion of their total sales in convenience goods. Depending on the size of the superstore and its location even other third-order centres (or certain of the shopping centres within these towns) can experience a fall in retail sales. The opening of a hypermarket on the edge of Caerphilly in South Wales in September 1972 was superimposed on an already well established shopping hierarchy which included within a radius of eight miles a second-order centre (Cardiff), a third-order centre (Pontypridd) and nine lower-order centres including Caerphilly itself and a suburban Cardiff centre. Studies of the impact of the hypermarket indicate that with the exception at first of Caerphilly town centre the spatial distribution of consumers using the store is sufficiently great that no one centre has suffered unduly (Lee, Jones and Leach, 1973; Lee and Kent, 1975; 1979). Moreover, it is difficult to distinguish the changes that have taken place because of, or irrespective of, the building of the hypermarket.

The decline in the number of food shops in the area cannot be blamed entirely on the hypermarket since it is a trend that has been occurring elsewhere for some time in response to supermarket development. Second, the changes in total spending reflect attempts by various centres, and not just the Caerphilly hypermarket, to promote consumer patronage. Certainly a facility with sales of £7.9 million in its first year and £9.4 million in its second, after allowing for inflation and increased spending from a new population, must have taken its trade from somewhere. The hypermarket undoubtedly acted as an intervening opportunity between Cardiff and many of the smaller centres to the north and as a result some Cardiff centres lost trade. However, the stores greatest impact was in Caerphilly town centre itself, and this will be considered in 2.6 overleaf.

24

As in the case of the large out-of-town comparison goods
centre there is a fear by retailers in nearby centres that a
superstore will seriously denude their trade. However, studies
at Caerphilly and elsewhere have shown that the hinterland of
a superstore can be as great as that for a second or third-
order centre: the hinterland for the Caerphilly hypermarket
and the very much larger centre of Cardiff are similar in terms
of travel distance, ability to attract trade across hinterlands
of lower-order centres and the frequency of shopping trip.
Moreover, it was shown in the Caerphilly case that the smaller
centres do not lose trade to the hypermarket on a permanent
basis; the degree of loyalty held for local shops is such that
it encourages only irregular trips to the hypermarket. The
loss of trade in the smaller centres is also selective since
the hypermarket attracts a higher proportion of young, large,
middle class and car-owning families. Also, the loss of trade
is proportionately greater from co-operative stores than from
multiples and independents (Thorpe and McGoldrick, 1974b).
However, even where there are no superstores, this loss is
taking place within the framework of the existing inter-urban
retail structure as these types of families are seeking
different shopping opportunities. It is important that
superstores be considered in the planning context as a further
type of preferred retail activity and location, and not simply
given a black mark because they are thought to upset irreparably
some unchanging status quo.

2.6 THE INTRA-URBAN RETAIL HIERARCHY

The central place concepts of range and threshold, seen in 2.5
above, also relate to the distribution of retail activities and
the hierarchy of retail centres within a city (Carol, 1960;
Berry, 1963), although the indices used in actual classification
of the centres may lead to a varying number of classes and
different systems of nomenclature. The highest-order centre is
the town centre, having the largest concentration of shops, the
highest proportion of sales in non-food items and serving in
theory the whole of the town and surrounding area. After this
the descending order of centres will depend on the size of the
town (see, for example, Carruthers, 1962; Thorpe and Nader,
1967; Guy, 1976). Cities over 100 000 and metropolitan areas
have a second tier of suburban and district centres which in
terms of their size and function may be more important than the
highest-order centre of many other towns. Suburban and district
centres invariably have a higher proportion of their retail
sales in food items and a more restricted range of non-food
items compared to the highest-order centre of that town, and
they have a more limited trade area. These second-tier centres
vary from fully-fledged town centres in the areas that have
been absorbed by larger cities (for example, Romford and
Uxbridge in Greater London) to planned district centres in
smaller cities (for example, the Cowley centre in Oxford and
Weston Favell in Northampton) and the many unplanned district
centres which have grown up over a longer period and often
appear as commercial ribbons along arterial routes radiating
from the town centre (for example, Reading's Oxford Road and
Portsmouth's North End). A third tier consists of neighbourhood

shopping centres varying in size from as few as eight shops
to as many as a hundred and catering mostly for the every
day needs of surrounding residents (solely or predominantly
food and other convenience items). The centres are spatially
well distributed and most consumers could walk to shop. In
cities under 100 000 district centres are often absent and
neighbourhood centres constitute the second tier. Beneath
this level are the isolated and small groups of shops,
providing a much more restricted range of convenience
retailing and varying from the once ubiquitous corner stores
in inner-suburban areas to the small parade of shops which
have been planned and built in recent years in outer-
suburban areas.

This intra-urban retail hierarchy has evolved since the
introduction of cheap public transport allowed a more
spatially extensive residential structure after the mid
nineteenth century and shopping in the town centre became
more inconvenient (Burns, 1959). However, that hierarchy
has tended to become institutionalised, and new retail
methods, organisation, functions and designs have been
developed (or are expected to develop!) within it. This is
perhaps because in the past the three or four-tier hierarchy
best fitted the overall needs of the majority of consumers,
provided maximum convenience and maintained the best
equilibrium (and non-competitive) situation amongst retailers
It still fits the needs of shoppers who are tied to public
transport use and who frequently do small amounts of
convenience shopping at local stores; various surveys show
that the British housewife is not following (at least not
very quickly) the example of her American counterpart and
shopping by car at one store once a week or less (I.P.C.,
1970; Daws and Bruce, 1971).

Since the Second World War British planning policy and
practice have reinforced the traditional intra-urban retail
hierarchy (Mills, 1974). Moreover, it will be seen in
Chapters 5 and 6 that at the local level, where the initial
design work is done and planning approval is given, there is
a strong input into the political decision-making process by
the business community who are keen to maintain the status
quo. Very often the decision-making body includes many
members of the business community, which makes for greater
ease in promoting various vested interests.

However, the retail hierarchy has been subject to change,
although some of this has come about indirectly as a result
of other social and economic changes. First, the isolated
and small groups of convenience stores have declined in
absolute and relative importance. It was shown in 2.1
that urban renewal, declining interest on the part of the
retailer, changing consumer preference and competition within
the industry removed many small convenience-good stores in
the inner areas of towns. Meanwhile, in outer-suburban areas
the planning of retail facilities on new private and public
housing estates almost totally excluded isolated stores and
invariably grouped a sufficient number of stores together
such that consumers would have the major necessities of

everyday shopping within easy reach. Planners have tried to be sensitive to consumer needs and provide the correct mix of shopping facilities; at the same time studies, such as that by Daws and Bruce (1971) in Watford, have shown the functions that consumers desire at the neighbourhood level and act as a further guide to planners. However, what consumers desire and what they actually use regularly may be very different. Furthermore, there may be insufficient threshold at that level to maintain the viability of a certain function.[1]

Second, since the Second World War there has been an unprecedented development, or redevelopment, of retail facilities in British town centres. The nature of this development and the implications for out-of-town shopping developments will be discussed in Chapters 5 and 6. In the present context what is important is that town centres have not only been growing in an absolute sense but also relatively at the expense of lower-order centres (Board of Trade, 1964; Department of Industry, 1975; Bennison and Davis, 1981). The trend towards multiple organization dominance in retailing, seen in 2.2 is a scenario that has been playing in the High Streets of British towns in both the convenience-good (supermarket) and comparison-good trades. Central and local governments have lent their support to this, in spite of the fact that in virtually all British towns and metropolitan areas the areas closest to the town centre have been declining in population.

This emphasis on town centre redevelopment and the increasing spatial separation between residence and store has resulted in various problems, especially relating to traffic generation and congestion, and subsequently there have been attempts by government and private industry to seek alternate locations for retail activity. The direction of government thinking, however, has clearly been in favour of developing district centres (the second tier of centres in an urban area) in order to protect and enhance town centres. One of the earliest examples of planned development was at Cowley in Oxford. The spread of residential development to the south and east of Oxford created a need for improved shopping facilities in that part of the city, and if a wide range of food and non-food items were provided there would be an opportunity to relieve some of the existing congestion in the historic city centre (City of Oxford, 1954). The Cowley Centre was built by the Oxford City Council, beginning in 1960, and by 1965 it had some 70 shops and 207 140 sq.ft. of floorspace. It was modelled on a new-town centre (and a North American suburban shopping centre) with a pedestrian precinct and free car parking on the fringes (National Economic Development Office, 1968). The size of the centre and its location in a growth

---

[1] In the Watford survey the most definitely required stores at the local level were chemist (98%), sub-post office (97%), grocer (96%), baker (95%) and butcher, greengrocer and newsagent/tobacconist (94%), while more than 50% desired a fishmonger, bank, hardware store, draper, shoe repairer, hairdresser and dry cleaner.

area were designed to attract consumers from a limited part of the urban area and not disrupt central area trading, hence the title of a district (or suburban) centre rather than a regional centre. But the emergence of a planned centre may disrupt trading at other centres in south east Oxford, and the National Economic Development Office study was designed to assess the impact of the Cowley Centre and what lessons could be learned for future developments.

Whilst population increase resulted in a need for more retail facilities, the Cowley Centre also took trade away from other shopping centres in that area of Oxford. The small neighbourhood centres on public and private housing estates were little affected, mainly because the areas were either hopelessly deficient in shopping facilities or had inconvenient or non-existent bus routes to the Cowley centre. Oxford City Centre lost customers for both food and non-food items, but this loss was more than made up by increased patronage from elsewhere, leading to new shopping development and further congestion in the city centre. The centres most affected were the two larger, unplanned, suburban ribbon developments (Cowley Road and Headington) where in four years one sixth of the stores closed down and it was feared that more might close as customers drifted to the Cowley Centre and retailers reacted to falling profits. These centres served immediate local needs but did not compete well for the longer distance customer, especially since car parking was poor and better retail facilities were available at the Cowley Centre for little or no extra effort involved.

From the point of view of town centre relief it would seem that the effect of the Cowley Centre was somewhat different from that intended; a Ministry of Housing and Local Government (1969) study also suggested that the district centre could relieve pressure on town centres. This could be done by allowing district centres to serve the convenience needs of between 20 000 and 40 000 people in adjacent suburban areas and thereby give the town centre a better opportunity to provide for comparison-good shopping for the whole area, convenience needs of those people who live in the inner city and the casual needs of people who work in the town centre. There is a need to make district centre shopping more attractive since there are invariably too many neighbourhood centres consisting of small shops straggling along arterial routes with limited trade areas, none of which may be good enough to attract multiple stores. Furthermore, a well developed series of district centres would lessen the need to carry out such extensive redevelopments in town centres. The Ministry study noted that much central area redevelopment focussed on supermarket shopping and that the attraction of food shopping from other areas had serious consequences in terms of traffic generation. A family of four requires approximately 60 to 70 lbs of food and drink (including containers and packaging) each week, and where weekly shopping is done on the basis of a major trip, it is almost imperative to have the use of a car.

An examination of structure and local plans show that the promotion of district centres is considered the norm in retailing planning. In spite of the slowness of formulating and approving these plans (at a time when there has been a veritable flood of planning applications for free-standing out-of-town shopping centres) it has been hoped, on the part of government and many sections of the retail industry, that the development of district centres will stem the tide of out-of-town centres. Certainly many new district centres contain superstores which could just as well have gone to a free-standing site elsewhere, and most of the district centres have been developed in areas of fast population growth where out-of-town shopping centres would have the potential for being very successful. However, it can also be argued that district centres and out-of-town shopping centres serve very different purposes, with the latter, for example, attracting consumers over a much wider area for a different type of good, and that both types of centre have a logical place in the retail hierarchy.

It is difficult to comprehend how the out-of-town shopping centre will be wished away so easily. In the South Hampshire Structure Plan (South Hampshire Plan Advisory Committee, 1972a; 1972b) some five new district centres, of between 70 000 and 130 000 sq.ft. (gross) each, were proposed on the outskirts of Southampton and Portsmouth in new suburban areas; but it was emphasised that the door should be kept open on proposals for large, free-standing shopping developments once their economic and social impact could be better assessed and should consumer attitudes change and/or more shopping facilities be necessary. However, the Committee's sentiments become outdated with the decision by the Department of the Environment (1972b) to allow a hypermarket of 124 000 sq.ft. (gross) to be built north of Southampton at Chandlers Ford. The local planning authority originally rejected the application since the hypermarket would limit options on the location, size and timing of district centre proposals in the Structure Plan, but the Secretary of State for the Environment overturned the local authority's rejection, stating that the hypermarket was not in a growth node area and therefore would not jeopardise the plan, yet the area was growing rapidly in population and needed new retail floorspace.

In some respects new and expanded district centres are similar to out-of-town centres in that they have engendered opposition from retailers in other centres. Both types of centre seek to improve consumer access to retail facilities, especially by car, but this must invariably mean a relative, or even absolute, decline in trade in nearby town and neighbourhood centres. The South Hampshire Structure Plan studies, for example, recognised that in promoting new and existing district centres there would probably be a loss of trade in the centre of Southampton and at the three main centres in Portsmouth (Commercial Road, Palmerston Road and North End), and, as shown above, the development of the Cowley Centre in Oxford unduly affected nearby older commercial ribbon developments. Many towns in the 75 000 to 125 000 population range have not only expressed opposition to out-of-town centres or superstores but to new or improved district centres in their suburban areas. It is feared that redevelopment and expansion of shopping facilities in their town centres may suffer, and in some cases the overprovision of shops and the already high vacancy rate may be made worse.

While district centres may receive opposition from traders and local politicians, they have received an official stamp of approval from professional staffs at the local and central government level who are concerned not merely with the provision of retail facilities but the wider ramifications of concentrating those facilities in town centres. But while the district centres may alter the balance of the intra-urban hierarchy, it does not seriously upset it in terms of either its size or location.

The free-standing, out-of-town centre, on the other hand, falls foul of the established intra-urban hierarchy in terms of size, number of stores and functions, trade area size and impact on the rest of the hierarchy; and this major upset of, rather than tinkering with, the system has resulted in opposition amongst not only vested interests but also professional staffs at various governmental levels. Out-of-town centres are rarely considered by planners at the formulation stage and are not designed to fit into an existing or planned retail structure in the least disturbing way possible. They are strictly commercial ventures proposed by private companies, and by the time planning permission is applied for, the centres have their architectural designs completed, tenants selected if necessary, and the site has already been purchased or is under options. It is at this stage that professional staff at the local level review the extent to which the out-of-town centre upsets the existing hierarchy. Most of the out-of-town proposals, concentrating on a superstore, are of the size and functional composition of a modest district centre, but the fact that the superstore's hinterland is spatially more extensive (see 2.5 above) means that their impact on any one centre in the intra-urban hierarchy is probably less than that of a new or improved district centre. The exceptions to this dictum occur where large superstore developments are proposed in slow or no-growth areas, where the existing or proposed retail structure is deemed adequate, or where the superstore is too close to an existing retail centre.

From the point of view of British superstore experience it would almost seem that the exceptions are the rule, and most planning applications are rejected on one or more of these grounds (Lee and Kent, 1976; 1978). Once a superstore is built it is often difficult to test a causal relationship between superstore success and retail decline elsewhere, especially as separation increases, although it is possible to be a little more definite when decline is rapid, dramatic and occurs in nearby centres. It was shown in 2.5 above that the hypermarket at Caerphilly had relatively little impact in an inter-urban context but its impact on Caerphilly itself was serious. The town centre, one mile south of the hypermarket lost eight of its twenty food stores between 1972 (when the hypermarket opened) and 1974, and in constant prices saw an absolute decline of 42 per cent in food sales (Lee and Kent, 1975). Whilst the number of non-food stores increased from 62 to 64 in this period, it masks the fact that total sales declined by a staggering 53 per cent. The impact of a superstore on the existing intra-urban retail hierarchy is selective and may also vary over time. In the Caerphilly town centre non-food stores could resist closing following a decline in sales whereas food stores were more vulnerable (perhaps because there were already too many stores and one large and successful addition simply forced closure on others). Within the food trades the superstore has taken a greater proportion of trade from one type of store than another (Rogers, 1974; Thorpe and McGoldrick, 1974b; Lee and Kent, 1975). The worst hit have been small supermarkets, or superettes, especially Co-op stores and the national voluntary groups located in both town centre and neighbourhood centres close to the superstore. The least affected are the large, multiple supermarkets and the small, independent grocery and specialist food stores; small grocery stores, even isolated corner stores almost adjacent to superstores, have maintained their viability through different opening hours, personalised service, delivery of goods and greater convenience in terms of walking distance, one or more of which can make up for higher food costs when compared to the superstore.

In the intra-urban context, the proposals for out-of-town free-standing superstore developments have caused near panic amongst retailers in other centres, especially town centre and nearby district or neighbourhood centres. Because superstores offer a wide range of non-food items the opposition to them is widespread from other retail organisations. Yet it is little realised that the impact of the superstore is selective and spatially well dispersed. Simply, the out-of-town superstore is seen as a revolutionary change, since it does not fit into the existing retail hierarchy, and opponents of change have been able to focus the public's and retailer's attentions on the issue. Meanwhile, changes have been taking place within the existing retail hierarchy which have had a more concentrated impact on the surrounding retail facilities; for example, the expansion of a High Street supermarket into a superstore, selling a wider range of non-food items, by the same firm that had perhaps been previously refused permission to develop an out-of-town superstore. The same degree of wrath is not incurred since the town centre's business community still feels that the centre as a whole has not suffered; if anything, it is naively believed that more and better retail facilities will result in every retailer improving his financial position.

2.7 CONCLUSION

In Chapter 2 an attempt has been made to view out-of-town shopping developments within the context of overall retail change. The moves towards free-standing superstores or medium to large regional shopping centres on the urban fringe

are not isolated events which will upset the status quo
regarding the inter-urban retail hierarchy. These developments
which are already well established in many parts of the world
especially North America and Western Europe, are a reflection
of changing consumer habits, modes of transportation and
population distribution; also, the retail industry has
undergone various institutional changes which have paved the
way to large shopping developments, including the decline in
the number of shops, the growth of larger shops, the growth
of multiple organizations and the increasing proportion of
business transacted by fewer and fewer companies, and the
involvement of private property companies and public
authorities in urban renewal and shopping centre developments

The store types and functional range found in out-of-town
shopping centres are not unique to those centres but are
merely an extension of similar developments taking place
within the existing retail hierarchy. Urban renewal in many
British town centres has often transformed them into North
American-style suburban shopping centres but without the same
amount of surface car parking. Meanwhile, many High Street
supermarkets of the 1950s and 1960s are being expanded in
terms of size and function into superstores, similar to those
in out-of-town situations. It is less the type of out-of-town
shopping development and more the actual location of that
development which is of concern to retail interests elsewhere
and whilst these interests are perhaps fully prepared to
tolerate change within the existing retail hierarchy (and
tolerance may come about through ignorance of the impact of
these changes), they view out-of-town developments by private
development companies rightly or wrongly as unfair and
damaging competition. To permit retail change but to restrict
its spatial expression reflects a protectionist attitude and
many of the arguments against out-of-town shopping centres
often demonstrate this quite openly.

3. The impact of out-of-town shopping centres and consumer preference

(Sufficient out-of-town shopping centres have now been developed in Britain, and numerous studies carried out on individual centres, for us to have a fairly clear idea of their impact on the existing retail structure and the type of consumer that is attracted to such an innovative feature.) Knowledge of both impact and preference plays an important part in the planning and approval of further developments by both private developers and public authorities. However, different groups in the decision-making process place different emphases on this knowledge. The private developer is primarily concerned with the viability of the proposed out-of-town centre, and the submission of such a proposal for planning approval is indicative of the fact that the centre will attract enough consumers to be a financial success. The planning process, on the other hand, is only marginally interested in financial viability, if only because enough examples abound that out-of-town centres are successful once completed. Of far greater concern is the damaging impact that the proposed centre may have on existing shops and the hardships faced by consumers using these shops should they fail; far less account is paid to the consumers who stand to gain by the development of an out-of-town shopping centre. Consumers in favour of something that has not yet been built do not constitute much in the way of an organised, vocal lobby. Besides different emphases placed on this knowledge, there is the further problem that local planning authorities often make decisions on the basis of limited or incorrect knowledge: proposals may be rejected because of what politicians perceive could be the impact on existing shops, not what is likely to happen given similar circumstances elsewhere.

In this chapter it is important to establish the nature of the impact of out-of-town shopping centres on the existing retail structure and secondly to examine the type of the consumer who is likely to switch his or her allegiance to an out-of-town centre.

3.1 RESEARCH STUDIES INTO OUT-OF-TOWN SHOPPING CENTRES

Unlike other types of retail development, out-of-town shopping centres have generated considerable controversy, and this in turn has led to numerous studies being undertaken by business, academic and government interests to assess impact and measure consumer preference (Thorpe, 1978a, table 2). The studies vary from those done for purely academic purposes to those which are used by private developers for promotional reasons or by government to help formulate policy and to make decisions on whether to allow certain developments It is no reflection on the quality of these studies that their use by private developers and public authorities has frequently been less than is perhaps desirable. Given the general climate of resistance to this type of retail innovation,which will be examined in Chapter 5, it is not surprising that private developers should underestimate the impact of an out-of-town shopping centre on the existing retail structure. On the other hand, public authorities, for example local planning committees, may choose to ignore all or part of such research studies or may be unaware of their relevant findings even though these may have been pointed out by the professional planning staff. Very often politicians may decide on the basis of a position held by a certain interest lobby which may have little or no understanding of the nature of out-of-town shopping centre impact, but which may tend to exaggerate the effects of that impact in order to persuade the local planning authority to vote down the proposal.

There are a number of other inherent weaknesses that relate to the effective use of these various impact studies. First, considerations of whether to approve or reject an out-of-town shopping proposal can be based on a number of other factors. Virtually all the research studies consider impact within the narrow confines of the retail structure and consumer choice. However, the development of an out-of-town shopping centre can have a considerable impact on other aspects of the social economic and physical environment. These wider consideration will be examined in the context of land use planning in Chapter 4.

Second, there is the problem of the validity of a study carried out at one location being used for the purposes of decision making at some other location. All the studies referred to by Thorpe (1978a) are of individual stores or locations and of necessity take into account certain local environmental conditions which may not be found elsewhere. However, given the large number of individual studies that exist it is possible to make certain generalisations about the impact of any new proposal, and it can be seen that at inquiries into planning refusals a good deal of credence is given to realistic information of the possible effects of a proposed development on the existing retail structure.

A third aspect, following from the above, is that even where
more general treatment (as opposed to individual store
research) has been carried out there is frequently a wide
variability in the results, thus upsetting previously held
assumptions and the validity of certain decisions that may
have been made. In what is described as the first study of
the trading features of hypermarkets and superstores in the
United Kingdom it can be seen that stores with similar net
or gross floorspace can have turnovers which vary by more
than 100 per cent (Jones, 1978). Yet it is frequently on
the basis of the floorspace of a proposed out-of-town
shopping centre that predictions are made concerning its
future turnover and thus the loss of trade that may be borne
by existing stores and centres. While the anonymity of the
various firms participating in the survey is protected, it
is noted that the variations in store turnover are more a
feature of differences in company trading practices than the
amount of floorspace, a fact known to retail firms but not
always fully appreciated by local planners.

Fourth, the various studies that have been undertaken are
predominantly after-the-fact assessments: 'before the centre
opened consumer behaviour' is frequently examined after the
centre has opened. There are few good studies undertaken
prior to an out-of-town shopping centre proposal being
considered by a local authority. It would be naive to think
that some studies, however rudimentary, are not done by the
major retail firms, but for reasons of not wanting to give
undue advantage to their competition or create any more
opposition than absolutely necessary, most of these studies
remain private.

Before-the-fact studies are of two types. The first identifies
the possible locations for centres (both in-town and out-of-
town) within a given area, or the merits of the one location
taking into account the availability of sites and access,
consumer demand, the inadequacy of local shopping and the
need to minimise the impact on existing retail outlets. An
example of this type of study is that commissioned by Glasgow
Corporation in the wake of a flood of applications for
hypermarket and superstore proposals (Marsley and Verrico,
1971); also, independent assessments are frequently made by
an inspector's appointee (assessor) at planning inquiries
conducted by the Secretary of State for the Environment.
However, the latter suffer from the weaknesses already
mentioned, namely that the assumptions may be based too much
on studies undertaken elsewhere.

The second type of study looks at present consumer habits,
the level of perceived satisfaction or dissatisfaction with
present retail facilities and may assess the need and demand
for out-of-town shopping facilities. Some of the resistance
to out-of-town shopping centres emanates from the fact that
many studies argue that there is little demand for such
facilities. An investigation into the possible effects that
a hypermarket in south west Sunderland would have on the
central area and existing district centres shows that only
20 per cent of those interviewed had ever visited an out-of-

town centre (Sunderland Corporation, 1971); although this is perhaps not surprising given the location of such facilities with respect to Sunderland. Moreover, only 39 per cent said they would definitely use an out-of-town centre, providing it matched the facilities of the central area, with a further 13 per cent saying they would occasionally visit such a centre. Hillman, Henderson and Whalley (1972) and Hillman (1973) state that the main reason a hypermarket is not needed in Sunderland is that convenience, or nearness, is the major consideration, especially for a grocery shopping trip; 43 per cent of the sample walked to the shop on the last trip, and 87 per cent walked to the shop on some occasion, far outweighing any other mode of transport. Yet they argue (although not altogether soundly) that if a hypermarket is built the local shops within walking distance will decline.

It is a major error of judgment to base out-of-town shopping centre decisions on present consumer shopping patterns and hypothetical questions about how consumers perceive new developments or what they may do in the event of the centre with its superstore or hypermarket being built. While there may be little clamouring from the shopping public or consumer groups for a hypermarket and apparent contentment with the present retail facilities, the introduction of such a facility will be an instant success, being greeted with approval from certain sectors of the population, and a preference for the innovative feature over the existing stores will quickly develop. Contentment is not something that is static, and it is relative; the emphasis on nearness, for example, can vanish in the light of significantly lower prices at a hypermarket and a strong promotional campaign (Taylor, 1972).

3.2   THE   TRADE   AREA   OF   OUT-OF-TOWN   CENTRES

It was shown in 2.5 and 2.6 that the extent of the trade area of the out-of-town shopping centre and the size and nature of population in that area are critical from the point of view of how the centre will influence the existing retail structure; although it was noted that it is difficult to distinguish the impact of an out-of-town centre on the existing structure from that of other retail changes that may be taking place, e.g. the expansion of central area supermarkets (Department of the Environment, 1978).

From the numerous impact studies that have been undertaken it is clear that the development of out-of-town shopping centres has resulted in very considerable changes in the traditional hierarchical relationships of trade areas. Out-of-town centres, with the exception of Brent Cross in London, are no larger than 150 000 sq.ft. (gross space) which may be considerably smaller than nearby town and district centres; moreover, the former have a larger proportion of floor space or sales devoted to convenience-food items compared to these other centres. With the exception of major cities such as Birmingham, Manchester and Leeds, the trade area of an out-of-town centre invariably extends over a greater area than most town or district centres. Thus, the impact of the out-of-town centre is more diffused spatially than the more traditional development taking place in a town or district centre. Whilst this is a factor that is well appreciated by planners, it seems to be so little understood by retailers and retail organisations in nearby centres. An examination of local newspapers in Colchester, for example, showed that the many superstore and hypermarket proposals outside the town drew considerable criticism from retailers in the town centre, which was out of all proportion to the likely impact the out-of-town centre(s) would have; but there was virtually no criticism from any of the other smaller centres within the likely trade area (approximately 15-20 mile radius), and some of these could have been quite hard hit. On the other hand, the approval of two Asda superstores in new district centres in Chelmsford and South Woodham Ferrers (approximately 20 and 25 miles from Colchester respectively) drew little criticism from the Colchester area. (There may, however, have been more criticism had there been better publicity by area newspapers and government consideration which extended beyond the district councils concered with the planning applications.) Yet since the two stores opened there has been a considerable advertising campaign in North Essex newspapers and no doubt some loss of trade from the Colchester area supermarkets. The distance-decay function of opposition does not reflect that of trade; the former is invariably excessive in nearby centres and falls off more rapidly.

The nature and extent of the trade area of out-of-town shopping centres depends on so many factors that all interrelate that it is very difficult in many instances to ascertain before a centre is built its likely extent, variations in penetration within the trade area and thus impact on the existing retail structure. The following factors can be seen as being important. First is the size of the out-of-town centre. Central place and retail gravitation theories suggest that the larger the size of the centre the greater the extent of its influence. Whilst this may be true for the traditional retail hierarchy in Britain, there are insufficient variations in the size of British out-of-town centres and perhaps too many other factors involved for similar assumptions to be made. However, from hypothetical studies undertaken (e.g. the University of Manchester Department of Town and Country Planning (1964) study of the Haydock Park proposal) and a knowledge of American and Canadian work (where the out-of-town, or regional, shopping centre is now very much a part of the traditional hierarchy), it can be suggested that size and geographical extent are related, hence the very real concern when large out-of-town centres are proposed and the lack of approval for all but one of them.

Second, trade area variations may reflect the type of product sold at out-of-town shopping centres. Thorpe (1978a) suggests that stores of the Woolco type and the Carrefour hypermarkets draw from wider areas than Asda superstores because of the emphasis of the former on non-food items. Theoretically, consumers travel further for non-food, as opposed to food, items; but some studies have shown that the ratio of food to non-food expenditures at the one store from different parts of its trade area can be similar, irrespective of whether the area is close or not to the store concerned (see, for example,

Thorpe and McGoldrick, 1974a). It may be increasingly irrelevant to differentiate between non-food and food expenditures in this way. The considerable cost savings of weekly bulk food purchases made at an out-of-town superstore compared to a local supermarket may encourage just as long a journey for food as for non-food items.

Third, the nature and extent of the trade area will reflect the composition of the existing retail structure. Many out-of-town centres have been developed in areas of large population and in close proximity to many existing centres, for example, the industrial areas of Northern England. While the higher-order regional and sub-regional centres, such as Manchester and Bolton, provide very superior shopping facilities many of the smaller centres are woefully inadequate. Their shopping facilities were a response to the demands of a local population, largely working class, which grew rapidly in the latter half of the nineteenth century. However, no one centre was able to establish sufficient dominance so as to provide the quantity and quality of comparison goods that were necessary Many of these small and medium size industrial towns entered the 1960s and 1970s with too many small, independent stores, offering a physically unpleasing environment and higher than average prices. Consumers endured this type of shopping environment not out of choice, but because the alternatives were seen to be a considerable distance away. However, an out-of-town centre, dominated by a superstore, in close proximity to a number of these small industrial centres suddenly provided consumers with such improved shopping opportunities that its success was virtually guaranteed. On the other hand, the weaker penetration of out-of-town centres in Southern England reflects a different population distribution both spatially and socially, a stronger and more varied retail hierarchy and a greater dominance by the multiple store and the High Street supermarket. In part the success of those out-of-town centres which do exist may be their draw in country town and rural situations where again shopping opportunities may not be all that consumers desire.

A fourth aspect to the trade area of an out-of-town shopping centre is the distribution and composition of the population. As will be seen in 3.4 out-of-town centres are not used equally by the different sectors of the population; and thus from the point of view of the extent and differential penetration of the trade area, the type of population can make a considerable difference. One of the key factors in this regard is the level of car ownership, and thus mobility. Thorpe (1978a) maintains that superstores and hypermarkets have a two-zone trade area. There is first an inner zone of about two to three miles radius from which the bulk of shoppers are drawn and where public transport and even walking may be important. The outer zone then extends a considerable distance, and can be almost exclusively associated with the car-using shopper. The attraction rate of the centre declines less with distance than is the case with traditional centres, reflecting not only the much greater use of the car, but its greater ease of use, compared to traditional centres. Whilst virtually all out-of-town centres can be reached by public transport, the number of

routes, frequency of service and areas having direct access
are considerably less than for most town and district centres.
The car, on the other hand, provides for lower travel times,
the comfort of door to door travel and the much greater
convenience of carrying bulk purchases. Thus, all other
things being equal, market penetration in this outer zone is
likely to be greater in areas where car ownership levels are
higher.

3.3 THE DIFFERENTIAL IMPACT OF OUT-OF-TOWN CENTRES

Even where the development of an out-of-town centre occurs
in an area of rapid population increase, there will be shifts
by the existing population from other retail outlets. However,
within a centre's trade area there are likely to be differences
in the degree to which existing centres and stores are
affected; moreover, it may not be those that are closest that
are most affected. Impact can be viewed in two different ways,
although both suffer from difficulties in the interpretation
that can be placed upon them. The first is to ask consumers
where they had previously shopped; but this merely tells you
who has deserted what and does not necessarily reflect how
the existing stores and centres are now coping with the
situation. Stores losing consumers to the new out-of-town
centre, may have gained consumers from elsewhere, and if not
they may have been able to reduce their expenditures such that
the reduced income still allows for the same profit margin.
The second approach is to examine the numbers of stores,
customer flows and estimated expenditures in the various
centres prior to and following the opening of the out-of-town
centre. However, the fact that the number of stores before
and after may be the same masks the financial hardships that
may, or may not, have been suffered: it is just that the
hardships were not sufficient to force closure. A drop in
the number of stores and estimated expenditures cannot
necessarily be blamed on the out-of-town centres. It was
stated in 2.5 and 2.6 that the existing retail structure is
undergoing change anyway, and it is not inconceivable that
some of these changes could contribute to the loss of stores
or custom.

An examination of the stores and centres previously used by
consumers shows little in the way of a consistent trend from
city to city. There is evidence to suggest that where the
patronage of a particular type of shop in an area is greatly
in excess compared to its overall national standing, there is
likely to be a greater loss of trade to the new centre. It
can perhaps be argued that this larger than average patronage
indicates a large number of consumers putting up with a
situation that they do not necessarily like, merely because
of inertia or because they like the alternatives even less;
but once a better alternative is provided, existing store
loyalty may amount to very little. In the Caerphilly example
in 2.5 it was the co-operative stores that suffered most
(Thorpe and McGoldrick, 1974b). In both instances these types
of shops were in an excessively strong local position compared
to Britain as a whole. But it must also be recognised that
superstores and hypermarkets in out-of-town shopping centres

offer greater price advantages over co-operative and small
supermarkets compared to the large multiple supermarkets
found in town and district centres.[1]

The location of the stores that suffer the greatest loss of
patronage is not always related to distance. Thorpe and
McGoldrick (1974a) and the Department of the Environment
(1976a) show that local shops and nearby neighbourhood centres
contribute fewer consumers or suffer a lower percentage loss
of trade than town centres further away. However, there are
more stores in the larger centres over which the loss can be
borne, and therefore it may be less critical to any one store.
Within the immediate vicinity of an out-of-town shopping
centre there can be considerable variation in the extent to
which existing stores suffer a loss of trade. Since the
superstore or hypermarket in an out-of-town centre is
principally used for bulk food purchases, it is likely that
existing stores, e.g. the small supermarket, concentrating
on this type of trade will suffer a disproportionate loss
(Thorpe, Bates and Shepherd, 1977). On the other hand, the
small independent store may be little affected by the new
store; the former's role is not for bulk purchasing (except
perhaps by a certain minority of households) but occasional
purchases (usually unplanned or previously forgotten, and
quality or specialty purchases). These small stores may
offer numerous other advantages which a superstore cannot
match, including local convenience, later closing, seven days
a week opening, alcohol sales (outside the legal hours!)
personal service and delivery of one's purchases. Furthermore
small stores had already established such a complementary
role, and thus a position of strength, when the town and
district centre supermarket was developed earlier.

Many of the impact studies that have been undertaken point
the way to more research needed on why existing stores close
down or lose trade after a nearby out-of-town centre opens.
It is all too easy to blame this on the new centre's superstore
or hypermarket by making a statistical (but not causal!)
connection. Very often the symptoms encouraging lost trade
or closure may be present anyway, and the superstore or
hypermarket merely helps, if it helps at all. Besides the
out-of-town centre it may be retail developments elsewhere
which are more to blame. The 1970s not only saw a rise in
the number of out-of-town centres, but an even more impressive
increase in the number and size of supermarkets and superstores
in existing town and district centres.

The Department of the Environment (1976a) study, for example,
indicates how difficult it is to assess the detrimental effects
of establishing an out-of-town centre. In looking at the
Carrefour hypermarket at Chandlers Ford it can be seen that

---

[1] It is interesting to note that in spite of research that
has been carried out, there are still those who fail to
recognise any differential impact on the part of superstores
(see, for example, Cassells, 1980).

the loss of three shops in Chandlers Ford itself had little
or nothing to do with the opening of the hypermarket: one
was the result of a liquidation by a national firm and the
other two involved trades that hardly competed with a
hypermarket. Information on spending in shops in Chandlers
Ford before and after the opening of the hypermarket is far
from accurate, but the decline over one year could be as high
as 26 per cent. However, it is difficult to apportion this
loss between the Carrefour hypermarket and other stores.
The opening of a large Tesco supermarket (42 000 sq.ft.) in
Eastleigh at the same time no doubt had its effect on sales
in both Chandlers Ford and Eastleigh; also, retail changes
in centres further away, such as Winchester and Southampton,
no doubt took trade away from the Chandlers Ford - Eastleigh
area. It becomes increasingly more difficult to assess the
effects of the Carrefour hypermarket as one moves further
away; in some instances, after allowing for sampling errors,
any increase in spending at a particular centre can be
attributed perhaps to various retail improvements at that
centre, while any loss can be attributed to people going
either to the Carrefour hypermarket or elsewhere.

There is a very real danger in not taking account of the many
other factors involved in the changing number of stores and
spending or turnover figures. In Chapter 2 this issue was
examined in the absence of any out-of-town superstore or
hypermarket. Changing consumer preferences, urban renewal,
company rationalisation (where fewer larger stores replace
small stores), entrepreneurial changes (e.g. death and
illness) and business inefficiencies have been important
factors influencing trade whether or not there is an out-of-
town superstore or hypermarket to lend influence. The changes
in the total number of shops in a centre within an out-of-
town centre's trade area may be quite small, but perhaps it
masks a considerable turnover in businesses, the majority of
which cannot be directly attributable to a new establishment
elsewhere. In Winchester town centre, for example, there
was a net increase of eight shops between 1974 and 1975 (from
175 to 183), but in the same period the total number of
businesses closing down or starting up was thirty (Department
of the Environment, 1976a, 90).

The timing of impact studies may, however, both under and
over estimate the long term influence of an out-of-town
shopping centre. A study undertaken too close to the time
of opening incurs two faults. The novelty and curiosity value
of an out-of-town centre, accompanied by considerable promotion
and opening sales, may attract people from considerable
distances, most of whom would probably be first-time shoppers
in that area. However, as time goes on the number of consumers
from such a distance could decrease: there is less disparity
in the sales' prices between the out-of-town centre and other
stores to warrant continued patronage, consumers may resume
previous store and centre loyalties (especially if existing
stores are able to adopt a better competitive stance) and
the frictions imposed by distance to the out-of-town centre
are seen to outweigh any advantages of visiting the centre.

In the Caerphilly and Eastleigh studies, where there was follow up work between two and five years after the centres opened, it can be seen that there was a decline in the proportion of consumers coming from more than ten minutes journey time away at Eastleigh and more than twenty minutes away at Caerphilly (Lee and Kent, 1975; 1979; Department of the Environment, 1978). The fall off in the proportion of consumers reflects the increasing localisation of the centres concerned. In the Caerphilly case this could perhaps be attributed to competition from more recent superstores (e.g. Asda at Dowlais) and a reduction in the price differential between the Caerphilly Carrefour hypermarket and other stores; in 1973 two out of three mentioned the price attraction of Carrefour compared to one out of three in 1978.

The second fault concerns the change in the number and turnover of stores at existing centres. Where a study is undertaken within a few months of an out-of-town centre opening, it may be too soon for a decline in a store's turnover to be catastrophic enough to force closure. Follow up studies are necessary to reveal the longer term picture, after existing store owners have had time to react and make decisions in their own best interest. Lee and Kent (1975), in their study two years after the Caerphilly Carrefour hypermarket opened, showed that since the first study (1973) the decline in trade and store closing in the nearby town centre had worsened.[1] However, the Eastleigh Carrefour hypermarket follow up study did not reveal anywhere near the same impact (Department of the Environment, 1978). Over a three year period the nearby centre of Chandlers Ford had a net loss of two stores (from 59 to 57); one of these was a small supermarket, but it could have been because the company concerned was undergoing a process of rationalisation anyway. In Eastleigh town centre there was a net loss of six stores (from 101 to 95), although this is reduced to three if allowance is made for four separate Co-op stores being remodelled as a superstore; the number of smaller food stores declined by a quarter (from 21 to 16), but this could be as much, if not more, a reaction to the opening of a large Tesco supermarket in the town centre.

The number of follow up studies is so few that it is hazardous to make any generalisations about long term impact. Furthermore, as time goes on it perhaps becomes more difficult to make the connection between the opening of an out-of-town shopping centre and its success on the one hand and the turnover performances and store closings in other centres, especially when these same centres exhibit their own successes in terms of new stores being opened. The contrast that is apparent between the Caerphilly and Eastleigh experiences may reflect the better population growth situation in the latter area softening the blow; although it is interesting to note that in the second

---

[1] See Chapter 2.6. It will be noted that the worsening situation was decidedly selective: the number of non-food stores in Caerphilly town centre actually rose between 1972 and 1974.

follow up study at Caerphilly, taken five years after the
initial one, the sales volumes in the town centre in 1978 had
recovered in real terms to four fifths of their 1972 level
(overall) and to three quarters in the food trades (Lee and
Kent, 1979). The opening of a Tesco supermarket in the town
centre no doubt helped this recovery, but it could also be
responsible along with the Carrefour hypermarket for the
further reduction of food stores.

Whether ot not out-of-town centres are located in areas of
population growth, and even owing for increased expenditures
by existing families through transfer from the non-retail to
the retail sector, the multi-million pound annual turnover
figure for an out-of-town superstore,[1] or for a town or
district centre superstore for that matter, must result in
trade being taken away from existing retail facilities. But
it can be seen that the impact is selective, both spatially
and by retail type, and reasonably well dispersed. Thorpe
(1978a) suggests that these new superstore developments are
not sufficiently large enough, nor the existing retail
structure so finely balanced, for there to be any catastrophic
reaction, although it is necessary to exercise greater caution
where either the nearby town is small in relation to the size
of the proposed development or there may be substantial
population loss. For the most part the problem has concerned
the impact of only the out-of-town centres with its large
superstore or hypermarket on the existing retail structure of
a nearby town or towns. But as the innovation spreads,
especially in large, high density population areas, it is
increasingly the case that the existing retail structure can
be affected by more than one out-of-town centre. The
development of a number of superstores in an area, whether
out-of-town or in-town, adds a further dimension to the problem.
Thorpe and McGoldrick (1974a; 1977) indicate that more
superstores do not lead to a catastrophic situation amongst
smaller outlets. In their studies of five superstore
developments in the industrial towns north of Manchester it
can be seen that a significant proportion of consumers at one
superstore had previously shopped at another; the most recent
addition, the Co-operative Superstore at Failsworth, had drawn
an astounding 62 per cent of its consumers from the other
superstores. As saturation point approaches in an area perhaps
it becomes more a battle amongst the retail giants, leaving
other parts of the system relatively unscathed.

3.4 SOCIO-ECONOMIC VARIATIONS IN CONSUMER PREFERENCE

The rapid growth of out-of-town centres in the 1970s and the
even larger number of proposals which failed to be approved,
reflect the potential of this type of retailing amongst the
shopping public. However, consumer acceptance and use are

---

[1] Jones (1978) shows that the annual mean turnover figure in
1975 for superstores and hypermarkets (both in-town and out-
of-town) in the 60 000 sq.ft. plus gross floorspace category,
for example, was £7.63 million.

far from universal, and many of the benefits of out-of-town centres that are claimed by entrepreneurs are not easily available to all consumers within the recognised trade area. Thus, acceptance might be greater if use was possible. The following variables are those that can most readily differentiate consumers:

Car ownership There is a far greater probability of a household owning one or more cars visiting an out-of-town centre compared to households not owning a car. As mentioned in 3.2 this results in part from the location of out-of-town centres and the ineffectual level of public transport to serve their trade areas. Most centres lie on or near perhaps only one radial bus route from the town to a suburb, outlying village or neighbouring town or city; in some instances there may be additional services resulting from cross-town routes (via the town centre), circular routes (avoiding the town centre), or multi-service routes from the town centre which branch after the out-of-town centre. In general, though, the out-of-town centre is served by far fewer services than nearby town or district centres, and most potential users arriving by bus would incur the added inconvenience of having to change buses somewhere. It can be argued that out-of-town centres could never serve their trade area by bus as economically as town centres: the former's trade area is more dispersed and the trip is almost solely for retail purposes. However, it must be wondered to what extent local government and transport authorities have encouraged bus useage: the expansion of routes to serve out-of-town centres is all too often seen as unduly favouring one entrepreneur over another and upsetting the retail balance. The fact that more bus transport is possible is seen from the fact that a quarter of all superstores and especially those not in established centres, run their own services (Neilsen, 1977).

The high proportion of consumers arriving at out-of-town centres by car,[1] the difficulties of reaching these centres by public transport and the fact that only 56 per cent of British households in 1976 owned at least one car have been major factors in opposing such developments. Furthermore, it is argued that car ownership alone does not mean that it will be used for shopping (Hillman, 1973). Women undertake most shopping trips, yet only one in five has a driving licence. Also, the ability to drive is not necessarily matched by 1) the availability of the car for shopping (the car could be used, for example, by the husband to drive to work) or 2) the desire to drive (many women cite medical reasons for not driving unless it is an emergency). Only in the two-car

---

[1] The actual percentage depends on the location of the centre with respect to the surrounding population (and thus consumers who could walk) and the nature of the bus service. Rarely is the proportion of car users less than 50 per cent; for most centres it is over 75 per cent, rising to 91 per cent in the case of the Eastleigh Carrefour hypermarket (Department of the Environment, 1978).

household is there considerable freedom to use the car for shopping, and a disproportionate number of these households are to be found at out-of-town centres.

The opposition to out-of-town centres on these grounds rarely acknowledges society's role in satisfying the needs and desires of those households who do have cars and who want to use them for this type of shopping. Moreover, such opposition ignores both the nature and implications of car ownership and some fundamental changes taking place in shopping habits. While the proportion of households owning one or more cars was only 56 per cent in 1976, this figure could rise to 65 per cent by 1985 (Department of the Environment, 1977a). Furthermore, the 56 per cent figure masks the considerable variations between the various regions of the country, within the one region and between different types of household. In 1971 the proportion of three (or more) member households (the nuclear family) having a car is 65 per cent, whereas for two member households it is 50 per cent and one member households 16 per cent (Department of Trade and Industry, 1973). For three (or more) member households car ownership varies from 42 per cent on Merseyside to 78 per cent in the Outer London area. However, retail habits vary between different types of household. The smaller (and especially older) the household the less the need for bulk buying of groceries at an out-of-town centre and the greater use made of shops in established (and probably closer) centres: not having a car, therefore, may be perceived by the household concerned as not constituting a problem. The fear expressed by Hillman (1973) that local shopping would be wrecked, thereby constituting a grave problem for the non-car owner, is wildly exaggerated and obviously has not happened. Where local shopping has declined, it is just as likely to be in an area far removed from an out-of-town shopping centre.

Fundamental changes are taking place in shopping habits which further enhance car oriented shopping. More women are obtaining driving licences. Indeed, the one in five figure above was an average, whereas for women under 50 it was one in three; the ratio can, therefore, only improve. Out-of-town centres (and superstores and supermarkets in existing centres) are almost always open in the evening usually until 8 p.m. (9 p.m. on Fridays); this results in greater ease of shopping for households where husband and wife both work and/or where the car is in use for something else during the day. In the Department of the Environment (1978) study almost one in three consumers using the Carrefour hypermarket at Chandlers Ford shopped after 6 p.m. The inability of the housewife to drive is perhaps less of a problem because of the greater involvement of men (even the whole family) in shopping. From a situation a generation before when husbands were rarely involved in food shopping, a 1974 study reveals 33 per cent of husbands engaging in this activity (I.P.C., 1975).

Social class The relationship between social class and the appeal of out-of-town shopping centres needs some careful consideration, since diametrically opposed viewpoints are commonly expressed. Planners, retailers (in other centres) and local government politicians are all too ready to believe that out-of-town centres appeal predominantly to the most mobile, car owning and large middle class households (the A, B groups as defined by the British census), since they are the groups who can best reach such locations. On the other hand, Thorpe and McGoldrick (1974a), in their study of four superstores in the north Manchester area, suggest that the impact of these stores is reasonably classless.

The experience of Thorpe and McGoldrick is matched by the image that out-of-town centres, superstores and hypermarkets have attempted to project. With certain exceptions[1] that image has been low to middle market, emphasizing reasonable quality, often brand name, merchandise at prices significantly lower perhaps than existing centres. The image of saving money, yet not jeopardising quality, is likely to appeal to all groups. However, what is possible and what at first is perceived may be quite different. In the hypothetical study of out-of-town shopping conducted in Sunderland (Sunderland Corporation, 1971) it was found that those people who had previously visited an out-of-town centre or who would visit such a centre, providing it had facilities that matched existing centres, were disproportionately found in the A, B and C1 groups.

When an out-of-town centre is developed and sufficient advertising and other forms of promotion are undertaken, it seems that perception can change particularly amongst the D, E groups. The actual distribution by social class group at any centre is more likely to reflect the location of the store, the nature of the area population and the levels of car ownership. The belief that out-of-town centres appeal to the middle class stems from the strong relationship between income and car ownership. The Department of the Environment (1976) study showed that where household income was in excess of £80 per week 92 per cent of the sample owned, or had the use, of a car; this compared with only 14 per cent where income was less than £20 per week. Therefore, the more eccentrically located the centre is and the more it depends on the car user, the greater the likelihood that it will draw a disproportionate share of its consumers from the higher-income groups. The social class variations between the stores that Thorpe and McGoldrick (1974a) found in north Manchester reflect the different types of population living within a certain distance of those stores. Also, the closer the store to a population who can reasonably be expected to walk to it and the better the bus provision, the greater use by the non-car owner and the greater the social class mix.

---

[1] For example, the Brent Cross shopping centre in north west London; Rogers (1974) noted an up-market image projected by the superstore at the Bretton, Peterborough, Centre, but this was not matched by significant social class variation.

Table 3.1

Household income, car ownership and the use of the Eastleigh Carrefour hypermarket

Weekly household income	Households with cars visiting hypermarket in past seven days	Households without cars visiting hypermarket in past seven days
	% of each income group	
Less than £20	10	2
£20 - £40	13	3
£40 - £60	14	3
£60 - £80	17	
Over £80	20	3

Source: Department of the Environment, 1976a. *The Eastleigh Carrefour, Minworth, Birmingham.* Research Report No. 16, (Department of the Environment, London).

However, the classless argument is not entirely convincing. Table 3.1 shows that the high frequency use of the Eastleigh Carrefour hypermarket is governed by access to a car; but more important amongst those who do own a car and who theoretically have the same opportunities to use the centre there is a considerable variation in the frequency of use according to income. A variety of factors could underlie these differences including the spatial distribution of the various income groups and thus the greater convenience of other retail centres, the availability of the car (the higher the income group, the greater the proportion of households owning two cars) and the need to use an out-of-town centre (the lower the income, the older and smaller the household is likely to be).

Household and family status   Out-of-town shopping centres differ from existing retail centres in terms of the age of the household, its composition and the actual nature of the shopping group. In both hypothetical and actual impact studies it has been found that a disproportionate number of young shoppers (in the under 50 category) are prepared to, or do, visit out-of-town centres. This reflects a number of issues. First, car ownership varies significantly between the different age groups; it is highest in the 30-40 category and by the over-60 category the proportion has declined by more than half. Thus as in the case of social class, the greater the dependence of the centre on the car user the higher the proportion of young families using it. Second, irrespective of car ownership, there is likely to be greater loyalty amongst older people for existing stores and centres whereas younger people, setting up new households and/or moving into new areas have yet to establish the same strengths of loyalty. Third, mobility decreases with age. Increasing physical infirmities and less mental ability conbine to place both real and perceived barriers to travel. Finally, the image of the out-of-town centre as principally advantageous to the one-stop, bulk-buying shopper may work against the older shopper, unless he or she is within easy walking distance and thus can view the centre as a new and better local shop. Otherwise, older people consume less than younger people and have less need for most durable products. Local, district and town centre shops may be perceived as just as convenient (if not more convenient if there is no car), and equally satisfying and competitive.

The composition of the household shopping at an out-of-town centre often contrasts quite markedly with existing retail centres. A larger than average number of three (or more) member households use the out-of-town centre. These households are more likely to be young and have access to a car, but also they are likely to gain the greatest advantages of price savings on durable goods and through the bulk buying of food. One argument against out-of-town centres is that they are not only inconvenient for older people, but also for families with young children. However, the studies by Thorpe and McGoldrick (1974a) and the Department of the Environment (1976a) for example, found this not to be the case. The picture of the harassed mother, burdened by pre-school age children, having to depend on local shops is a misnomer. Whilst many may use local facilities, especially for topping-up, and may find them convenient, many more find the out-of-town centre equally convenient or more advantageous for other reasons, such that there is little appreciable difference in the frequency of the two groups (with or without young children).

The nature of the shopping group (the observed family or non-family group at the centre) may in part account for the ease by which households with young children can use out-of-town shopping centres. Comparisons between the Eastleigh Carrefour hypermarket and four existing retail centres in the area showed that the out-of-town centre attracted a far higher proportion of two member (adult male and female) groups than the existing centres; there was a corresponding much lower proportion of adult females shopping alone (Department of the Environment, 1976a). At the hypermarket 23 per cent of shopping groups were accompanied by children, whereas at the other centres the figure varied from 11 to 14 per cent. The greater incidence of the family group, easing the traditional burden of the housewife and treating shopping as much a pleasure as a duty, has become the hallmark of the out-of-town centre.

3.5 THE ATTRACTIVENESS OF OUT-OF-TOWN CENTRES

Much to the chagrin of their opponents, out-of-town shopping centres, once developed, rarely experience anything but success in their retail operations. As we have seen these centres carve out an extensive, but selective, trade area, appealing in the process to certain types of consumer. Their success in part depends on the promotion of various trading practices and features which result in their being markedly different in many instances from existing retail centres

48

(Mills, 1974;   Gilham, 1976;   Unit for Retail Planning Information, 1976). The following identify in order the major attractions for consumers:

Prices A variety of practices result in out-of-town centres either selling goods more cheaply than existing centres, or being perceived by consumers as doing so. Underlying this are the cheaper land and construction costs of out-of-town sites, the economies of scale in their operation and the no-frills approach to retailing, e.g. warehouse-like structures, display by means of open sided boxes which reduce labour costs in stacking shelves, etc. (The last two also apply to superstore and discount store operations in in-town locations). Price cutting on goods and aggressive advertising of this through the media are the major images that consumers have of this type of centre, although it must be recognised that different entrepreneurs approach the matter in different ways.

When asking consumers their reasons for shopping at out-of-town centres, lower prices invariably figure the most prominently (Lee, Jones and Leach, 1973;   Thorpe and McGoldrick, 1974a;   Department of the Environment, 1978). However, consumers have varying attitudes to the question of prices. Thorpe and McGoldrick (1974a) found that the significance of price as the main reason for patronage was greater amongst older people, lower-class shoppers and those with large families. It is perhaps ironic that the first two groups here, who stand to gain more by lower prices than younger and higher-class shoppers respectively, are so often at a greater disadvantage from the point of view of reaching the out-of-town centre.

There is evidence to suggest that cheaper prices do not continue to be as important a reason for attracting consumers (Department of the Environment, 1978; Lee and Kent, 1979). Critics of out-of-town centres have argued that the price differential between those centres and existing centres is greatest when the out-of-town centre is first opened in order to attract and establish a clientele; but once this has been done and the slashed prices of opening sales have been ended, prices begin to rise and the differential is reduced. It must be added that the differential could just as likely lessen as existing shops react to the out-of-town centre by reducing their prices and becoming more competitive, a situation that helps the shopper who cannot or does not want to use the out-of-town centre. The monitoring of prices at out-of-town centres and nearby shops is a costly and complex procedure and the results so far fall short of those desired. However, Thorpe and McGoldrick (1974b) found that one year after the Caerphilly Carrefour hypermarket opened its prices on various brand items were 11.3 per cent lower than the average for the area and 8.7 per cent lower than the cheapest multiple supermarket. Sixteen months later the difference had declined to 8 per cent and 6.4 per cent respectively, chiefly because of competitors lowering their prices. This is supported by tentative research undertaken by Social Community Planning Research (Unit for Retail Planning Information, 1976). The follow up study undertaken at the

49

Eastleigh Carrefour hypermarket showed that whereas 55 per
cent of consumers identified lower prices as their main reason
for going there in 1975, only 37 per cent did so in 1977
(Department of the Environment, 1978). This could reflect
changing differentials in prices between the hypermarket and
existing shops, but also the greater proportion of consumers
in 1977 coming from the local area; it can be seen that local
consumers place far greater importance in locational convenience
than in lower prices.

Location   In spite of the location of many out-of-town centres
in areas and on sites that are more divorced from the population
compared to existing centres, various factors concerning
location show up strongly in the reasons why consumers use such
centres. Included here are the relative location with respect
to area of residence, and perhaps more important, convenience
- the ease by which consumers can reach the centre. It has
been found that those people who walk to out-of-town centres
cite location as a more important factor in their shopping
choice compared to people who come by car (Thorpe and McGoldric
1974a). Similarly, people who come from a short distance away
irrespective of transport mode, tend to place far greater
emphasis of location and convenience compared to consumers
who travel greater distances (Department of the Environment,
1978). Given the increasing emphasis on car oriented shopping
and the diffused nature of the out-of-town centre's trade area
location and convenience may take, on less importance as a
reason for shopping choice or a different meaning (e.g. differe
criteria for evaluating the convenience of one centre vis-a-vis
another). From the point of view of the latter, the
concentration of supermarkets and durable-goods stores in town
centres and ensuing congestion that has resulted from increasin
car useage have meant that out-of-town centres much further
away may increasingly be seen as more convenient perhaps
because of an easier journey by fast main roads.

Shopping environment   The third group of factors relating to
the attractiveness of out-of-town shopping centres concerns
they layout of the centre, its overall atmosphere, the degree
of ease in shopping there and the level of satisfaction
achieved. Critics of out-of-town centres, albeit some years
ago, maintained that the shopping environment is foreign to
the British shopper who would much prefer the traditional
style of shopping set out in the Sunderland and Watford studies
(Sunderland Corporation, 1971; Daws and Bruce, 1971). However,
foreign and unacceptable should not be confused with
unfamiliarity; any innovation is foreign, and presumably at
one time out-of-town centres were 'foreign' to North American
and continental European shoppers too (these countries are the
chief culprits for introducing this type of centre and
exporting it to Britain).[1] It seems that once the out-of-town

---

[1] In the heat of xenophobia it is not appreciated by some that the
superstore or hypermarket is not a North American feature since there
the supermarket and discount-department store functions (i.e. food and
non-food) have traditionally been separated. The first hypermarkets
were introduced from Europe in the early 1970s. The American or
Canadian out-of-town centre is of the type seen at Brent Cross or at
planned district centres such as Cowley (Oxford) and Weston Favell
(Northampton).

centre is introduced British shoppers are only too prepared
to cast off traditional ways and follow their North American
or European counterparts. Meanwhile, it should be remembered
that many Comprehensive Development Areas in town and district
centres are modelled on the out-of-town experience (the sole
difference sometimes being the substitution of surface for
multi-storey car parking); yet, in the case of the former
one hears little or no comment about a 'foreign' environment.

The chief environmental factor is shopping under one roof and
the one-stop shop. This refers to both the comforts of a
climatically controlled, clean and bright atmosphere and the
ability to obtain easily a whole range of everyday goods (both
food and non-food) on the one trip, most likely at the one
cash register. A further aspect is the convenient shopping
hours. Many centres close completely one day a week (usually
Monday) and have evening shopping hours on most, if not all,
other days. It is an environment which encourages many of
the social and economic trends that are taking place in
retailing, including the bulk purchasing of goods, the once
a week (or less frequent) major shop, the involvement of the
family in shopping and the combining of shopping (for
necessities) with pleasure (browsing for possible purchases,
eating out etc.).

Parking A final set of factors relates to the use of the car
at the out-of-town centre. However, considering the high
proportion of consumers who arrive at the centre by car it is
invariably the least important of the four major factors.
Ignoring those who do not arrive by car, this may reflect
consumers taking it for granted that out-of-town centres can
easily accommodate even peak hour traffic loads, or consumers
who are prepared to put up with any shortcomings; also, the
advantages of these centres over existing centres relate more
to other issues than those of parking. It is often suggested
that a major attraction of out-of-town centres is the
availability of free parking, contrasting markedly with most
town centres, but in the study of the Eastleigh Carrefour
hypermarket only 4 per cent of consumers identified it as a
main reason for shopping there (Department of the Environment,
1978). Of far greater importance was the ease of parking,
taking into account presumably the nature of approach roads,
the availability of vacant spaces and the proximity of that
space to the shop itself. Unlike the other three factors
parking is frequently viewed as one of the major disadvantages
about an out-of-town centre, but since the reasons for this
are so similar to parking in town centres it probably will
not result in consumers going elsewhere to shop. Many out-of-
town centres underestimate the number of parking spaces needed
to accommodate peak loads, necessitating expansion later but
resulting in the meantime in congestion. On the other hand
the provision of more surface parking spaces merely exacerbates
the ease by which the consumer can then reach the shop.

3.6 CONCLUSION

It has been shown that in spite of the many fears of their opponents, out-of-town centres provided by private entrepreneurs on free-standing sites have not led to the complete demise of existing shops and retail centres. Numerous impact studies have been conducted in the last ten years to give retailers and planners a reasonable idea of the effects of a new development on the existing retail structure although there remains the problem of comparability and transportability of the research, especially in its specific details. The trade areas of such centres are first of all more extensive than those of existing centres of equivalent size, and second the impact on that trade area can be differentiated according to factors such as the relative location of the centre, population distribution and variations by type, the nature of the existing retail structure and the degree of personal mobility. However, the problem remains of what changes in the retail structure can be directly attributed to the opening of an out-of-town centre or to the many other changes taking place within the existing centres. There is little doubt that out-of-town centres have been readily accepted by the shopping public, although that acceptance is far from universal. The key to one's using such a centre is often car ownership or car availability which in turn leads to a disproportionate share of consumers being younger, middle class and coming from larger households. Finally the impact of out-of-town centres is a reflection of their attractiveness to consumers. The factors most readily identified relate to cheaper prices, location and convenience, the shopping environment and parking. In spite of the many attractions of out-of-town centres and their acceptance by consumers, considerable opposition has been raised by politicians, professional interests and other retailers concerning their development. The nature of this opposition and the wider issues of out-of-town centre development will be considered in the next three chapters.

4. Land use planning and conflict

on the rural-urban fringe

Retail change cannot be viewed in isolation from other
socio-economic activities. The growth of new shopping
developments and the decline or modification of existing
shops not only influence the overall retail structure and
consumer behaviour: the location of these activities and
their use frequently conflict with other land uses and
threaten the efficient functioning and amenity value of both
the urban and rural area. In the case of the out-of-town
shopping centre the land use conflict is heightened by the
fact that such centres rarely feature in the detailed
planning proposals by the local authority; this is not
surprising as the centres, unlike town and district centres,
are almost entirely conceived by the private sector alone
and initially at least are not related to other types of
urban development (e.g. surburban residential development).
In the absence of any long term strategy from the private
sector it is almost impossible for the local authority to
plan for an out-of-town centre, even if they were willing,
unless the authority is involved with the centre as part of
some comprehensive urban expansion proposal (and thus the
out-of-town centre becomes a district centre). The result
is that planning permission is often sought for out-of-town
centres in areas that are not presently used for retail
commercial purposes, or indeed zoned for that purpose. The
granting, or not granting, of planning permission thus hinges
on a series of evaluations, often very subjective, concerning
the effect of the transfer of the land to retail commercial
purposes on the original actual or intended use, the impact
of retailing on adjacent land uses and the wider effects on
the urban environment should development take place. The
planning mechanism in Britain is such that opponents of out-
of-town centres (on the basis of the competition that would
be generated) can effectively mask their bias and self
interest by expanding upon matters relating to land use and
physical planning.

It can be seen that problems associated with out-of-town
shopping centre development have received considerable
attention in the planning process, reflecting a long tradition
of physical planning, together with the legal requirements
of the Town and Country Planning Acts, 1947 *et seq.*; these
in turn reinforce various cultural attributes concerning the

orderly growth of settlement, its separation and the
maintenance of community identity, preservation of agriculture,
the amenity value of the countryside and minimising the
conflict between urban and rural lifestyles and values. The
out-of-town centre is criticised because it represents a
considerable departure from existing land use, consumes a
sizeable quantity of land, is highly visible and not altogether
attractive, and its use results in a series of locational and
behavioural conflicts. In this chapter three major areas of
conflict are pursued, all of which have jeopardised both the
general acceptance of out-of-town centres and the approval of
individual centres: these refer to the protection of the
countryside against urban encroachment, traffic hazards and
various site characteristics.

4.1 URBAN ENCROACHMENT AND THE PROTECTION OF THE COUNTRYSIDE

There has been considerable concern in British planning circles
over a long period about the spatial aspects of urban growth,
especially the ways in which that growth conflicts with
agriculture, rural amenity and access to the countryside.
The tremendous urban growth since the beginning of the
nineteenth century, and more specifically the spatially
extensive growth in areas such as Greater London in the inter-
war period, highlighted these conflicts and the contemporary
inadequacies of British planning law (see, for example, Thomas,
1970; Hall, Gracey, Drewett and Thomas, 1973; Hall, 1974).
A series of measures and accompanying legislation since the
Second World War have been designed to arrest this situation
and redirect urban growth, both nationally and regionally,
including the Distribution of Industry, New Town, Town
Development and Town and Country Planning Acts. All of this
legislation is multi-purpose, but a strong underlying theme
in all of it has been the need to protect the countryside
from the worse excesses of suburban growth and urban sprawl,
particularly in the fastest growth areas of Southern England
and the Midlands. Conflicts still arise, however, because it
is not feasible in terms of social justice to contain urban
growth within some existing limits: resulting residential
densities were felt to be unacceptable and the needs of non-
residential activities could not be well satisfied. Thus,
in the post-war period there are still considerable demands
made upon the countryside to contain various urban related
activities, and a number of new forces operating upon society
have added to, or modified, the nature of that demand,
including, for example, the expansion of airport functions,
the growth in car ownership and the increased demand for
'exurbia' living and the growth of industry, warehousing and
shopping on the urban fringe. Whilst legislation has allowed
the protectionist lobby a better means of preserving the
countryside, the same legislation is also having to cope with
a whole new set of circumstances, which could hardly have been
forseen in the 1930s and 1940s; thus, these protectionist
groups are constantly having to resist or divert new pressures
upon the countryside.

The opponents of out-of-town centres on the grounds of encroachment upon the countryside constitute a very varied group. Profession organisations, including planners, and local government politicians, have generally not taken any overall stand, but at the local level most proposals are likely to raise objections from these two areas. However, planners and politicians invariably couch the objections in terms of the wider planning issue: the out-of-town centre disperses urban functions, encourages decentralisation of activities and longer journeys, threatens the functional and physical separateness of town and country and weakens the concept of self-contained balanced communities and the viability of existing town centres. Various organisations who oppose out-of-town centres have either a vested interest in the countryside or verge on the conservative romantic whose mandate is often to preserve the status quo against all urban intrusions. These range from national groups, such as the Council for the Protection of Rural England, to specialist rural based organisations (for example, farmers and amenity groups and the various county and village residents' associations. Finally, there are the groups whose expertise or political involvement in planning matters is limited and who have little direct interest in protecting the countryside from urban encroachment. These include town ratepayers organisations and businesss groups, such as Chambers of Trade, both of which have other more important objections to out-of-town centres; the protection of the countryside argument is used to strengthen their case or to divert attention away from group self-interest which is likely to be threatened should the out-of-town centre be built.

Out of town shopping facilities are viewed with particular concern, not only because they consume considerable acreages of land[1] but they may act as a catalyst for other types of development, which either may not be desired or would be better located elsewhere within the urban area, and conflict with present or proposed land uses. A number of distinct land use planning issues are involved:

Divergence from the Local Plan   As a result of the Town and Country Planning Act 1947 and subsequent Acts the use, or intended use, of all development land is prescribed in the short term. A proposed out-of-town centre, originating as it does from the private sector, rarely conforms to present uses or future land allocations. Either the land is designated to stay in its present state, or it is proposed by the local authority that the land be used for some other urban purpose.

---

[1] A 100 000 sq.ft. gross floor space centre will have set aside anywhere from 10 to 20 acres of land. The exact amount depends on the size of the land holding(s) bought, the arrangement of the store on the site and the ratio of car parking spaces to sq. footage.

The possibilities of changing the land use designation to accommodate an out-of-town centre vary first according to the type of present use. The greatest resistance to change is put up where the site is underdeveloped, is surrounded on at least one side by undeveloped land, is scenically attractive and there are no official proposals for development. A second situation is where various urban uses are either already in existence or are proposed in local plans, and thus the protection of the countryside may not be compromised. It seems curious, therefore, that from a land use planning viewpoint a further urban use, such as the out-of-town shopping centre, should not be accepted. The processes that have led to its decentralisation are very similar to those of industry or warehousing; but while the last two have been adequately accommodated in purpose-built, urban fringe estates, retail activity of any form, let alone the large store or centre, is invariably treated unfavourably. In many instances permission is sought to change the use of a building from industry or warehousing to retailing or mixed retail-warehouse uses, or to redesignate the proposed use of the land, in the same way; but permission is usually refused on the basis that such conversion would unduly affect future opportunities (Department of the Environment, 1977a). However, it is frequently the case that too much land has been set aside for industrial and warehousing purposes in the past, especially given the absolute or relative decline of the manufacturing sector of the economy in many parts of the country (Department of the Environment, 1982a). Also, retailing may offer more employment and generate more income in the local economy compared to other commercial uses, and is certainly better than vacant buildings or derelict land. In the light of planning refusal the demand for urban fringe retailing has encouraged unauthorized conversion of premises and the seeking of loopholes in the Town and Country Planning Act concerning what contributes a warehouse or retail use.

There are instances where out-of-town shopping centres, or smaller retail activities, are viewed as improvements over existing urban land uses. Much land and also many buildings, especially in the major industrial areas of the country, are vacant or in a state of dereliction; and thus, the possibilities of returning land and buildings to non-urban uses or converting to other urban uses are frequently of considerable concern. The greater occurrence of out-of-town centres in these older industrial areas, compared to Southern England for example, is partly the result of local authorities not wanting to pass up the opportunity of the private sector doing the job of land reclamation for them. Many of the early superstores were accommodated in converted premises in this way but in recent years, however, the trend has been distinctly towards undeveloped sites and purpose built premises.

A further aspect to changing land use designation in a local plan relates to the notion of prematurity. This occurs where the local authority refuses a planning application for an out-of-town centre on the basis that the present time is not opportune. The last fifteen years have been a time when both

local government reorganisation has taken place and local
authorities have been changing from old style Development
Plans to Structure and Local Plans. There has been a desire
in many places to make no substantial changes in land use
until this process is complete. Furthermore, the proposals
from the private sector may conflict with public proposals
for future urban growth. The opposition to the Eastleigh
Carrefour hypermarket in part resulted from the fact that it
was not included in one of the growth nodes set out in the
Structure Plan (Department of the Environment, 1972b; South
Hampshire Plan Advisory Committee, 1972b). When appeals have
been held into local planning refusals the prematurity
argument has not always been supported (Lee and Kent, 1976);
it has been suggested that local authority planning could
well incorporate new types of shopping opportunity, and that
it is unfair and impractical to restrict changes until plans
are approved. Beside it is all too often the case that the
prematurity argument is used against out-of-town centres more
than against other types of urban development.

Prematurity is also seen in arguments concerning shopping
centre need. Many planning applications are refused because
at the time there is sufficient floor space available in
existing centres and already approved expansions, given the
size of population, its spending habits and the nature of the
existing shopping opportunities (see, for example, Department
of the Environment, 1975c; 1975d). This points to a very
traditional method of estimating need and takes no account
of changing needs which cannot be met by existing or proposed
retail space. Moreover, local authorities are being selective
when they speak of prematurity in the retail sector: they
have rarely been as reluctant to approve central area retail
changes which create excesses of space.

The extension of the built up area   One of the many issues
indicating a divergence from the Local Plan relates to the
physical boundary of the urban area. This boundary has either
been set or is proposed in most Local Plans, and many planning
applications for out-of-town centres would constitute an
extension of the boundary and perhaps contribute to other
types of urban development and thus further extensions. The
physical limits to an urban area have never been, and can
never be, permanently established, but local authorities can
establish preferences on the direction of urban expansion,
encouraging one fringe area while totally restricting another.
The area to be restricted may have well defined physical
boundaries which can act as a buffer between urban and rural
development including limited-access highways, water courses,
sudden breaks of slope, park areas, valuable agricultural
land and large, long established land holdings where urban
sprawl has been resisted; some of the uses in this area
could be part of a designated green belt. It is felt that
there is more to be gained by restricting urban development
here compared to an area where the physical boundary is less
distinctive and the amenity or resource value of less note.
The numerous out-of-town centre proposals on the edge of
Colchester were refused in part because they conflicted with
what was termed the logical boundary or urban development in

the forseeable future (Department of the Environment, 1977b).
To the north west and west side of the town this was defined
by existing development, a river valley and a limited-access
highway and its approach roads. Had any of the proposals
been on the north east side of the town, where development
had long before leap-frogged the valley and further developmen
was being encouraged, there may have been a greater chance of
approval. (Eventually one of the companies proposing a
superstore co-operated with the local authority and built in
a new district centre in this latter area.)

It can be seen that the extension of the built up area is not
merely an urban question but relates to the nature of the area
over which the development is to take place. The greatest
resistance to urban expansion is generally found in those
areas which are considered best for preserving in their natural
state or for retaining their present rural uses.

The preservation of agricultural land   The present state of
agriculture and the nature of soils and other physical
attributes for an agricultural economy have been important
factors in the promotion of urban containment and have been
expressed through action groups, such as the Garden City
movement, various commissions (Barlow and Scott) and post-war
planning legislation. It can be argued that there has been
undue concern about the preservation of agricultural land to
the detriment of efficient planned growth of urban areas and
the adequate supply of development land at reasonable cost.
Far less consideration is given to the fact that it is
possible to consume more agricultural land for urban uses
and yet increase productivity. The minority report of the
Scott Commission, among others, pointed to evidence of
technological innovation leading to increased output, although
of late there are doubts as to the long term advantages of
doing this (Champion, 1978). However, in spite of this,
proposals from the public or private sector for expansion in
rural areas where agriculture is strong invariably meet
resistance from an agricultural or amenity lobby; although
it is debateable whether it is agricultural productivity that
is threatened or the whole way of life engaged in by the rural
resident, which includes the visual rewards of country as
opposed to town.

The out-of-town shopping centre has been generally criticised
by various levels of government and interest groups because
it is a wasteful user of land as well as having the potential
for consuming acres of good farmland. Where good farmland is
involved the matter is considered in the course of granting,
or not granting, planning approval (Department of the
Environment, 1982b), but rarely is it a major factor in
rejecting an out-of-town centre. Lee and Kent (1976; 1978)
in their studies of planning inquiries into shopping centre
refusals note that the quality of agricultural land is not a
major consideration and is less important than factors
concerned with rural amenity.

The protection of the green belt   As part of the policy of
urban containment green belts have been proposed or approved
around all or part of most urban areas. Green belt areas, if
rigidly supported, have a very restrictive effect on various
land uses. Earlier urban developments, now surrounded by
green belt, are sometimes forced into higher density
redevelopment; and new urban development is encouraged to
leap-frog the green belt to towns and villages beyond, thereby
increasing commuter distances. Meanwhile, some green belt
areas may be sufficiently cut up by main roads and railways,
impinged upon by surrounding residential areas and hard to
operate from an agricultural standpoint that their retention
is more a matter of community separation (however tenuous)
rather than an attempt to promote certain non-urban functions.

Many out-of-town shopping centre proposals conflict with green
belt policies, and the tendency has been for such proposals
to be refused unless an exception can be justified or there
are other more compelling reasons why the centre should be
developed. In refusing green belt sites, government officials
could suggest less contentious sites which do not conflict
with green belt policies and which are just as accessible to
consumers. However, opposition to retailing outside the
traditional or planned retail hierarchy is such that suggestions
of this nature are rarely forthcoming. While it is government
policy to protect green belts (Department of the Environment,
1977a), there has been a lack of consistency in what constitutes
a justifiable exception or a more compelling reason. The
proposal to build a Carrefour hypermarket at Minworth near
Birmingham, was initially rejected by the local authority,
but at a subsequent inquiry the inspector stated that the
green belt objection was minor since other development had
already taken place in the same area (Department of the
Environment, 1975e). Although the Eastleigh Carrefour
hypermarket was in a green belt area, the inspector at the
inquiry found this acceptable because the site was at least on
the edge of the built-up area, and besides, green belt policies
here were in a state of flux (Department of the Environment,
1972b). Meanwhile, similar sites have been rejected because
they would unnecessarily intrude into the green belt (see, for
example, Department of the Environment, 1981a; 1981b). Other
more compelling reasons can be seen to be just as subjective,
for example convenience for food shoppers. This formed the
basis for approval of out-of-town centres at Minworth (Department
of the Environment, 1975e) and Thanet (Department of the
Environment, 1975f) but was not sufficient to warrant an
invasion of green belt lands at Shenstone, Lichfield (Department
of the Environment, 1973) and North Benfleet, Essex (Department
of the Environment, 1975c).

Attitudes towards out-of-town centres and the rate at which
the innovation has spread may be modified as green belt
policies change. British post-war planning exemplifies the
difficulties and frustrations of trying to establish an iron-
clad green belt around urban areas. While access to the
countryside may be enhanced (this may be a red herring in an
era of unprecedented increased mobility through car ownership)
and agricultural and rural amenities are preserved, these have

taken place at the expense of efficient urban development. Decentralisation of urban activities has been lopsided in favour of the residential function and its location is all too often isolated rather than peripheral to existing urban development, thereby encouraging increased expenditures on transportation. The adoption, for example, of the growth corridor concept, rather than the urban/green belt or urban 'doughnut' concept, would release green belt land adjacent to existing urban development and create wedges of green belt between the corridors. It can be argued that this would give even better access to the countryside. Certainly the urban growth concepts in many of the new Structure Plans, and more specifically the *ad hoc* decisions by planning inspectors (supported by the Secretary of State for the Environment) favouring development in green belts, point the way to a weakening of existing policy.

The green field location   The acceptability of out-of-town centres in land use planning terms is also related to their actual location with respect to the existing urban area; moreover, this is an important consideration irrespective of whether the location is in an approved or proposed green belt or not. The major concern with actual location rests on whether the out-of-town centre site is 1) a logical extension of the built up area or proposed as part of a new growth area or 2) physically unrelated to existing or proposed development by being on a 'green field' site. The Department of the Environment's (1977a) Development Control Policy Note, in giving guidance to local planning authorities, stresses the problems that could result should a 'green field' site be approved. These included the intrusion into open country, the demands made on the road system and public services and the precedents that may be set for further developments which it may not be possible to resist once the shopping centre has been built. Local planning authorities have, however, been very cognisant of this type of development, since to permit it would endorse some of the worse excesses of urban sprawl and to turn the clock back to an era when planning controls were weaker or non-existent.

Proposals for out-of-town centres would indicate that the most obvious 'green field' sites rarely get beyond the local planning committee stage. Of the appeals to the Secretary of State and resulting inquiries only one, the Woolco proposed near Twyford in Berkshire, was a 'green field' site (Department of the Environment, 1974b). The site was physically separated from any built-up area; however, it was sufficiently well located not only to threaten the trade of a number of nearby centres, but possibly to attract other residential and commercial development such that a coalescing of communities could take place on the east side of Reading.

4.2   TRAFFIC   HAZARDS

A major concern when considering out-of-town shopping centres has been the extent to which the extra traffic generated by the centre would be detrimental to the existing highway network conflict with other activities and cause an overall loss of

60

amenity. A number of separate problems can be seen here
which involve one or more of the local planning authorities,
other retailers and various residents' and amenity groups.

The local planning authority has the responsibility to assess
the impact the centre will have, and whether the road network
both in the immediate area and in the centre's major trade
area is capable of carrying the increased traffic. Traffic
not only relates to shoppers' cars but also the workforce at
the centre and the commercial vehicles serving the various
stores. Apart from the roads in the immediate area of the
centre there are few instances when the road network is
considered incapable of taking the required extra traffic.
The exceptions relate to the larger comparison-goods centres
(Lee and Kent, 1976). In two of these cases the proposals
were ultimately turned down, and in the third (Brent Cross)
a number of new roads were approved to relieve pressure on
existing roads. Of far greater concern to a local planning
authority are the roads in the vicinity of the centre. It
can be seen that the extra traffic generated by the centre
can cause a variety of problems, particularly at peak shopping
periods; and the fact that the centre may face a major trunk
route is not necessarily any guarantee that there will be no
traffic problems.

First, a local planning authority is keen to see that access
routes to the centre have sufficient capacity to take both
existing traffic and the additional shopping traffic in the
peak flow periods. Trip generation models are fairly
standardised practice to estimate both the number of cars and
their distribution on the access routes, although it may not
be possible to get too accurate a prediction because the
breakdown of consumers by transport mode is not as easy to
predict beforehand. A second aspect concerns the problems of
actual entrance and exit. It may be that surrounding roads
are quite capable of taking the extra traffic volume, but
junction situations and right hand turns, for example, into
the site can cause queueing on access routes, congestion and
thus inconvenience to existing traffic and increased accident
rates. It seems that problems of approach rather than actual
road capacity contribute more to a local authority refusal.
However, it is not beyond the realms of possibility to undertake
road improvements to help capacity and approach, particularly
the latter which is invariably cheaper anyway. But it must
be remembered that many local authorities are against out-of-
town shopping centres *per se*, and therefore they are hardly
likely to go out of their way to plan for and bear the expense
of road improvements or to encourage others to do likewise.
It is a situation very similar to that seen earlier in the
context of bus transport provision.

A problem which is addressed by local planning authorities
but more especially by resident and amenity groups relates
to the conflict between increased traffic and other activities;
this conflict has the potential of increasing personal accident
rates and property damage, and therefore leading to increased
insurance, medical, legal and associated expenses. Also,
there are the possibilities of more visual, noise and air

61

pollution, and the resulting loss of property value and amenity.

The traffic volumes generated by an out-of-town centre may b such that both road capacity and the nature of the approach routes are more than adequate. But technical statistics hav not been allowed to hide the fact that the local road networ on the rural-urban fringe, with the exception of inter-urban trunk routes, evolved to serve a rural, agricultural and or suburban residential population; in terms of standards and design it often cannot cope with a large import of commercially oriented traffic without unduly affecting other activities. One of the persistent worries concerning out-of-town shoppin centres is that they alter traditional journey-to-shop movemer which the road network and the public transport system are designed to fit. Instead there are greater traffic movement than planned for on minor country roads and residential stree in suburban areas and outlying villages. The Woolco proposa near Twyford, for example, drew considerable opposition from parish councils, residents associations and various amenity groups because of the unacceptable level of traffic along narrow village streets and housing estate roads and the proble this could cause to individuals, property and the urban and rural environment (Department of the Environment, 1974b). Again, when local authorities are opposed to out-of-town shopping centres little attempt is made to minimise conflict by altering traffic circulation (stopping up streets to frustrate through movement in residential areas, one-way traffic on country lanes etc.) and thus encouraging movement to the centre on the more major roads.

4.3 SITE CHARACTERISTICS

An out-of-town shopping centre proposal raises a number of issues which can best be classified as site characteristics, and to varying degrees land use planning and planning contro are influenced by these. In some instances local planning authorities are faced with issues which are very objective i nature or which directly or indirectly affect other urban activities. On the other hand, at the other extreme the mer suggestion of an out-of-town centre can provoke a series of subjective and perhaps highly emotional responses concerning its effect on the wider urban and rural environment. Rarely can it be seen that decision making at the local or central government level will result from site considerations alone. But at the local level various site considerations have been important in planning as a whole over a long period, and whe a proposal for an out-of-town centre is made public in an area these considerations come to the fore and strengthen the opposition to the proposal. While the eventual refusal of a particular proposal rests on more important criteria, it is not uncommon for many of the issues relating to site to have been raised somewhere in the planning process. The followin identify the more important concerns here:

Servicing implications The development of an out-of-town centre can influence the effective use of existing services. Two of these, the road network and approach routes to a cent

and public transport provision have already been raised;
further services which must be considered are the major public
utilities of water, sewers, gas, electricity and telephone.
Where an out-of-town centre proposal is made in an area that
is not designated for urban development, it is likely that
essential services are either lacking entirely or inadequate,
and there are unlikely to be any plans to provide for or
improve such services. However, if the centre constitutes an
extension of the built-up area, it is often possible to tap
major trunk services without too much difficulty, given of
course the right political environment. The chief difficulties
arise with the 'green field' site. To attempt to control
development on the basis of inadequate or non-existent public
utilities is a strong argument: if services are extended to
a 'green field' site, then intermediate areas are also
serviced and therefore subject to new development pressures.
Urban physical boundaries often conform to service boundaries:
to expand the one is to expand the other. It is difficult,
politically, to deny further development. Moreover, the extra
development may be needed to justify the cost of the service
lines to the 'green field' site.

Car parking   The provision of adequate car parking at an out-
of-town centre to meet peak demand is in fact a servicing
problem. On the other hand the extensive amounts of surface
car parking that accompany such centres has led to one more
of the many environmental issues, therefore the need to treat
this issue separately. Thorpe (1978a, table 6) suggests that
relatively little variation exists in the amount of car parking
provided by the different centres in spite of their varied
locations and the variety of sources of information that both
developers and local authorities depend upon. Common practice
is to base car parking provision on the sq.ft. of gross retail
space or sales area. However, Thorpe (1978a) states that
suggested ratios of parking spaces to 1000 sq.ft. sales area
have been too low, since they are based on work carried out in
areas where a smaller percentage of households own cars. In
the case of the Brent Cross shopping centre, the inadequacy of
car parking at the time of opening reflected the far higher
proportion of shoppers who were expected to arrive by bus and
underground; when this did not materialise, a multi-storey
car park was built to provide extra parking that was needed
(Shepherd and Newby, 1978). With some exceptions out-of-town
centres have tended to provide adequate car parking. In this
way retailers need not fear that the car-owning shopper will
be turned away. Moreover, the availability of land for a
generous parking provision and its cost are usually better than
at existing centres. Also, by providing adequate parking there
is little or no risk that planning permission will be refused
on the basis of shoppers having to use neighbouring roads and
residential streets for parking at peak times.

Even where there is little chance of unsightly and dangerous
parking in neighbouring areas there are often other environmental
issues associated with parking. Many opponents of out-of-town
shopping centres have argued that the generous provision of
parking spaces encourages car useage, detracts from bus useage

even where the services are more than adequate and conflicts with the need to conserve energy resources. Furthermore, the very high proportion of the site area that has to be given over to surface car parking raises the cry that a valuable and irreplaceable resource or rural amenity is lost for all time. It is interesting to note that employee car parking at an urban fringe industrial estate does not raise the same cry. Also, it assumes that the shopping centre car park is built on rural land; in the older industrial areas of the country it is often the case that an out-of-town centre even with its acres of tarmac is an improvement over what existed before and allows for valuable private investment in the rehabilitation process. It is, of course, not beyond the realms of possibility of having an attractively designed car park; for example, incorporating lines of trees and various ground cover and building materials to break lines of sight and surface expanses.

Shopping centre structures It has been mentioned before that out-of-town centres are alien to tradition in Great Britain. One aspect of that tradition seen here is that these centres do not as a rule conform to existing on-street or off-street shopping centres in terms of their design, use of materials, siting and landscaping. Whilst the Department of the Environment (1977a) Development Control Policy Note draws attention to questions of design, one must question the extent to which developers and local planning authorities are actually concerned; and therefore one can appreciate much of the opposition that is levelled at out-of-town centres on design grounds.

Compared to existing centres and many of their Comprehensive Development Area schemes and even the North American regional shopping centre, British out-of-town centres, especially those dominated by the one superstore or hypermarket, represent for the most part a very dismal picture in terms of overall contribution to urban and suburban amenity. Shopping centre design tends to emphasise convenience and a very functional approach, whilst keeping within the bounds of safety regulations, and little thought or money is given by the private developer to creating a structure which is aesthetically pleasing: perhaps the developer thinks there is little financial return on aesthetics. The result has been a shopping centre environment which both inside and out closely resembles the factory or warehouse. (Indeed, many out-of-town centres are operating in former factories or warehouses.) Evidence of the hard sell functional operation of so many of these centres is everywhere to be seen; for example, no natural light (windows take away from the area that could be useful for shelf space), bins of canned goods rather than neatly stacked shelves (reduced labour costs) and minimal decor (reduces capital costs). From the outside the centre is usually very visible, surrounded as it is by acres of parking space. Little or no use is made, for example of plants and trees, outside furniture and fountains and other water bodies to relieve the sterile, functional landscape. The buildings invariably show little relief from box like structures with the emphasis on prefabricated materials and minimal attempt

64

at individuality in architectural design and the use of
building materials. Local authority response has in fact
been to accept this sterile, functional environment as perhaps
the best that can be expected from the development industry;
besides, it is merely an extension of existing industrial and
warehouse areas in the suburbs which are similar in many of
their visual aspects. Moreover, to expect more of shopping
centre developers is to run the risk that they might seek
alternate locations in other local authority areas where fewer
impediments are placed in their way. This contrasts markedly
with central area shopping developments where a far greater
emphasis is placed by local authorities on architectural design
and how well the proposed development fits in with existing
buildings and the overall historic character of the area.

Visual intrusion A final aspect, combining both the structure
itself and the parking around it, is that the out-of-town
centre constitutes a visual intrusion. Whilst it may not
actually interfere with the operation of various activities
on nearby properties, it could however offend the eye of those
who live in adjacent residential areas or who enjoy in some
way the rural amenity either in the area that will be lost or
close to it. An out-of-town centre is probably such a contrast
from what existed on the site before, or compared to adjacent
land uses, that it would matter little how well it was designed
and landscaped: indeed, any urban development may be objected
to in like fashion. The major exceptions, as mentioned above,
would be those areas where the overall amenity and visual
intrusion would be improved by the centre's development.

All too often what offends the eye is closely associated with
economic considerations. There is the very real fear by
adjacent homeowners that the visual intrusion of an out-of-
town centre, accompanied by the noise and interference of
traffic, increased litter problems, greater risks of accidents
and so on, will result in a decline, either relatively or
absolutely, in residential property values. This is in part
reinforced by the limited extent to which homeowners have
obtained a reduction in the rateable value of their property
once a centre has been developed.

Government response to the visual intrusion problem has been
threefold. First, and quite simply, it has not recognised in
some instances that there is any problem. This can result
from there being little or no objection from adjacent residents;
or the local authority chooses to ignore local opposition in
favour of more important considerations which should determine
whether a centre should be built or not. In doing so it is
realised that local opposition is frequently a form of
protectionism or self-interest: there is no objection in
principle to out-of-town centres so long as they are built in
somebody else's area.

Second, local authorities have most often responded to out-of-
town centre proposals by rejecting them. However, rarely is
this done on this basis of their visual intrusion and the
objections raised by neighbouring homeowners and others who
use the area. At best it is a secondary issue, but it lends
weight to the refusal argument.

Third, where government has given permission for out-of-town centres to be built it is possible to put conditions on approvals such that developers will attend to certain questions of visual intrusion. Certainly various shopping centre design manuals exist such that it is possible to learn how to hide or ameliorate the worse effects. However, to be realistic, a 10 to 20 acre site with a shopping centre structure and surrounding parking is going to be a distinctive feature in the urban or semi-urban environment. Whilst it is possible to have more pleasing and less functional architecture (the planned district centres in suburban areas point the way to what can be done, given less brash commercial overtones), it is more difficult to know how to lessen the visual impact; for example, too much tree planting in a car park would hinder the view of motorists and increase accidents, whilst a move to multi-storey or underground parking would add prohibitedly to costs and jeopardise any out-of-town proposal unless there was a far greater input of public monies.

4.4 CONCLUSION

The out-of-town shopping centre poses a number of land use planning problems and conflict situations which have contributed in varying degrees to the rejection of the majority of proposal. The most important problem is the clash between the out-of-town centre and the strong tradition of protecting the countryside against urban encroachment. Since most proposals originate directly from the private sector, it is unlikely that they conform to local planning controls and the present and future designation of land on the rural-urban fringe. Such proposals are most likely to clash with either the physical boundary set for the urban area, valuable agricultural land, the establishment of a green belt or the objections to isolated 'green field' locations. The planning process has shown, however, that these traditions of protecting the countryside are often 'sacred cows' which hinder efficient urban development. More recent planning proposals for the countryside near urban areas, plus the overturning of planning refusals for shopping centres in the green belt, point the way to some modification of traditional beliefs. A second area of concern is the traffic hazard that is likely once the centre is developed. Additional traffic generated can be detrimental to the existing highway network and the access routes in the immediate area, causing a conflict with other activities and an overall loss of amenity in nearby suburban and rural areas. The third problem relating to site characteristics rarely surfaces as a major concern and does not provide strong grounds for objecting to out-of-town centres, but it lends weight to refusal arguments and has been important for so long in colouring personal and official opinion against these centres. Included here are the problems of service provision, car parking, the shopping centre design itself and the visual intrusion all of this causes.

5. The out-of-town centre and resistance to retail change

After land use planning problems, a further reason for the
slow growth of out-of-town centres is related to the strong
resistance that proposals usually receive at the local level
(Gayler, 1979); this resistance is borne out of fear, real
or imaginary, of the likely impact of the centre on existing
retail trade and has resulted in the large majority of
proposals for private, free-standing centres or single large
stores being rejected. The planning process in Great Britain
allows for the very adequate expression of opinion, especially
against some proposal. It is possible through reports of
council and committee meetings, newspaper reports, and
inspectors' statements from planning inquiries to examine the
nature of this resistance to change, in terms of who is
involved and the reasons for their opposition, and how
individual and group attributes are translated into decision
making and the eventual acceptance or rejection of the proposal
(see, for example, Blowers, 1980). Through the deliberations
on any proposal it is invariably the case that the opposition
is numerically and politically superior to the proponents.
Apart from the developers themselves few proponents speak out,
and there is little attempt officially to gauge overall public
opinion. On the other hand, no two proposals which are
similar are likely to receive the same type or intensity of
opposition. Also, it should not be assumed that because a
proposal is vigourously opposed that it will be rejected by
local or central government; conversely, an absence of
serious opposition rarely means an easy passage for acceptance.

This chapter will first of all examine the various groups who
are involved in this resistance to retail change and the ways
in which they can make their influence felt. Second, the
planning process will be analysed to indicate the effectiveness
of this resistance. Third, attention will be paid to the
important themes which underlie this opposition. Resistance
focuses on the two notions that there is little or no demand
for new retail facilities, especially of the type proposed,
and that the proposed out-of-town centre will constitute too
damaging an innovation on the existing retail hierarchy. All
too often the objections as stated, as in the case of
objections on land use planning grounds, mask a series of
vested interests in preserving and enhancing the status quo,
in particular the protection of the interests of the small,

independent retailer, the promotion of the traditional
retail hierarchy in both the inter and intra-urban context
and a resoluteness not to jeopardise other types of retail
development, as well as wider urban changes, that may be
taking place.

5.1 THE GROUPS RESISTING CHANGE

There tends to be a large measure of consistency from one
out-of-town shopping centre proposal to another in terms of
the groups that are likely to register their opposition and
work actively to see a proposal defeated. However, the
submission of a proposal for planning permission does not
necessarily mean that opposition is going to emerge. Groups
who would most likely oppose could be weakly organised or
non-existent in the area or might not view the proposal as
a threat; while local government politicians, weighing up
the pros and cons of a proposal, could in fact favour it for
reasons other than its likely impact or damaging effects.
There are three major areas of opposition which have been so
effective in the past few years or so in frustrating or
blocking attempts by developers to build out-of-town centres:

The retail sector The thought of out-of-town centres has
particularly raised the ire of other retailers in the
community; they feel that it is unfair competition, since it
is a type of retail trade that they cannot enter. Also, since
it is likely to jeopardise their business, it is thought
therefore that their customers are likely to suffer from
decreased shopping opportunities, especially if they are unable
to use the out-of-town centre. The worst fears are expressed
by the small, independent retailer, many of them owning only
one store, and are usually expressed through retail organisation
such as chambers of commerce or trade covering the whole
community, as well as branches of these or traders' organisation
in individual shopping centres. The large comparison goods
centre proposed at Wolvercote, north of Oxford, shows the
typical business protest than can be expected (Department of
the Environment, 1972a); included here were the Kidlington
Chamber of Trade (the nearest community) and Oxford Chamber
of Commerce and two shopping centre organisations (Summertown
in the northern suburbs of Oxford and Cowley District Centre
to the south east). However, the vigour with which business
opposition is pursued can vary considerably. When the regional
shopping centre at Brent Cross in London was proposed, various
local chambers of trade expressed their disapproval. However
when the matter can to a planning inquiry, only one chamber
was represented and then its legal counsel called no witnesses
(Department of the Environment, 1970). It had become apparent
that many businessmen did not view Brent Cross as too great a
threat since it was likely to take trade away from Central
London (the West End) rather than adjacent centres.

On the other hand, the larger, independent retailer, for
example the family-run department store, and the multiple
firms are far less likely to resist the development of out-
of-town centres. They tend not to be members of local chamber
of trade, and if so, are not as vociferous in their objection

First, their experiences have been such that they have little to fear from out-of-town centres. Most multiple firms have benefitted from the increasing proportion of total trade realised by their sector of the retail economy, a success story which has been at the expense of the independent retailer and the co-operative societies. Moreover, the number and size of out-of-town centre proposals are not regarded as large enough to make a serious impact on the multiple firms. Second, it is the multiple firms themselves, and more especially the supermarket-oriented businesses, which almost entirely make up the out-of-town shopping centre activity. If a firm not presently engaged here felt its central area business seriously threatened, then it is highly likely to take steps to arrest the situation (by perhaps becoming more involved nationally in out-of-town locations or improving the competitiveness of various central area businesses). The multiple firms have their own national and regional trade organisations; and therefore it is unlikely that one in the group (with a town or district centre location) will oppose another's initiatives in a nearby out-of-town centre, if only because the tables could be reversed in some other area.

The vast proportion of multiple firms in the non-food trades have rejected or not even considered out-of-town locations, co-operating closely with local authorities in town and district centre schemes, and it may be thought that they have little to fear from those firms who do venture forth. However, the neutral stance taken by this majority may change as more large firms become involved in out-of-town locations, and success there is translated into a changing share of the market. The recent development of SavaCentres in Britain, a joint operation between Sainsbury's (a traditional supermarket firm) and British Home Stores (principally a clothing store firm) shows how the latter can break away from a High Street location and a narrow set of product lines and be part of the out-of-town superstore success story.

Professional groups The groups have become involved in the out-of-town shopping centre debate in two ways. First of all there has been considerable discussion by various groups of professionals in academic journals, the press and at the seminar level. This has involved government officials, planners, architects, estate management, engineers and the various social science disciplines, and has been an attempt to analyse the social-economic processes underlying changing retail location, monitoring change and the problems associated with it, and aiding the decision-making process. The attitudes held by these groups vary from opposition of the type shown above by Hillman (1973) to caution (Unit for Retail Planning Information, 1976) and support (University of Manchester, Department of Town and Country Planning, 1964). They reflect a need to look at the wider retail implications of any new development and a fear that development on the edge of the built-up area will inextricably alter the patterns of urban movement and growth and harm the rural environment. Parallels are frequently drawn between what could happen in Britain and what has happened in North Amerca and a desire is expressed not to follow the latter example. Certainly there is little sentiment to bow to the pressures of a forceful development industry with their claims of untold benefits for the consumer. A note of optimism in the professional field has come about as a result of the very extensive impact research that has been carried out in the 1970s (Thorpe, 1978a, table 2). Work by the Retail Outlets Research Unit and others has helped to dispel the worst fears about out-of-town shopping developments. It is unfortunate that the influence of much of this work does not extend past professional groups and is little understood in some of the areas where it really matter notably the independent retailer and the local politician. This is not as serious as it may seem, however, since the professional is very much involved in the planning process at the local level.

The second area of involvement of the professional group is a very direct one in the planning process. In the course of approving or rejecting a request for planning permission variou members of a local planning authority's professional staff will examine the proposal in terms of first the legal requirements under the Town and Country Planning Act, various other Acts and Orders where necessary and approved Plans, and second, various objective and subjective evaluations of its beneficial and detremental effects. This may be followed by final professional advice to the authority by the Chief Planner Professional judgment at this level has been very much divided. First, there is a need for the professional to judge each case on its own merits. Therefore, while he or she may hold an overall viewpoint that is favourable to out-of-town centre development, it may be necessary to reject a proposal within one's own area because it fails to meet certain criteria. The reverse situation is also true; for example, a planner's general opposition to out-of-town centres where a proposal enhances, rather than damages, the environment and there is clearly a need for more and improved shopping facilities. In either case personal preference is waivered in favour of the wider public good. Second, decision making at the local level can also be unduly influenced by opinions held by professional staff. These can, of course, be both in favour or against such proposals, but when one's opinion of the general case is allowed to influence a particular proposal then a measure of unprofessionalism is being injected into the planning process. By so doing it is hoped perhaps to either mould political opinion (since it is local politicians who have the final say, should there be no appeal) or give politicians the view they want to hear. To a degree the resistance to out-of-town centre development and the slow diffusion of the innovation compared to other industrialised countries reflect a conservative attitude on the part of the professional. This is borne out of a strong desire to keep to many of the traditional concepts concerning urban renewal, urban containment and protection of the countryside, and second, to link physical land use planning to the wider concepts of social and economic planning, for instance the easy availability of a strong, competitive retail system to the underprivileged members of society and the extent to which this could be jeopardised by allowing a car-oriented shopping centre on the urban fringe.

70

Local politicians   The third area of opposition, which has been so effective in stifling out-of-town shopping centre development, concerns the local politician. Politicians meeting in committee or council have the sole power to vote for or against a proposal, except that a negative vote can be challenged by a developer before a planning inquiry, and in some instances a proposal can bypass the local politician process by being called in by the Secretary of State. This issue has rarely divided local councils on purely political party lines: both the Labour and Conservative parties have easily found themselves in the opposition camp. Labour councillors object to out-of-town centres because they believe it would interfere with local shopping and therefore unduly effect those people who especially depend on it, including the old, the infirm and the poor. Conservative councillors, on the other hand, see out-of-town centres as placing undue hardship on the town's small businessmen, many of whom have invested in their stores and developed under a different set of conditions. However, both groups have just as easily found reasons to support out-of-town centres, although the number of cases in far fewer. Labour tends to support the benefits of cheaper prices and increased employment opportunities, while the Conservatives value the notions of private enterprise and an unwillingness to have the state intervene in competition within the private sector.

Since planning is initially done on a local, or district council basis, it is possible for there to be rivalry between the politicians of different local authorities or within the one local authority. Thorpe (1978a) suggests that prior to local government reorganisation of 1974 many local authorities, particularly in Northern England, granted planning permission to out-of-town centres in order to prevent the loss of purchasing power of its population to neighbouring centres. In turn it was presumably hoped to gain purchasing power from surrounding areas. There is also a town versus country argument, since many of the new district councils after 1974 resulted from the amalgamation of boroughs with urban and rural districts. Town politicians see an out-of-town centre as a logical extension of the built up area, providing in a sense a district centre to a new suburban area and bringing about improved shopping facilities and a lessening dependence on car travel to the town centre. Meanwhile country politicians see an out-of-town centre as a visual intrusion into the countryside and affecting the viability of small town and village shopping in adjacent areas.

While the potential for political rivalry exists, it was shown in 2.5 above that it does not invariably take place. Whilst politicians in neighbouring local authorities wish to protect their own shopping centres from competition, the politicians in the area where the out-of-town centre is proposed wish to do likewise. A good deal of rivalry may take place in other areas of retailing where the public sector intervenes (e.g. the competition resulting from Comprehensive Development Area schemes in adjacent communities). However, the out-of-town centre is so heavily dominated by the private sector and the dangers to the status quo are perceived to be so great that local politicians of different political persuasions and from different authorities can find very easy grounds for a common opposition front. So much so that there is little or nothing to be gained by an out-of-town centre developer trying to play one local authority off against another by threatening to locate in a neighbouring area.[1]

An important consideration in this resistance to retail change at the local level is the close association between the small businessman and the Conservative councillor. The opposition to out-of-town centres from the former is easily communicated to the latter through either the social connection or the fact that many Conservative councillors are small businessmen. Although these councillors may not be in businesses that stand to be affected by the development of an out-of-town centre, they can more easily identify with those small businessmen who will be affected. On the other hand, the shopping centre developer and the multiple firms which locate there have virtually no connection with the local political scene: if there is any connection it is likely to be at a national level, for example, through giving to party funds or having MPs on boards of directors or retained as legal counsel. This business-political alliance at the local level is a contributing factor in the spatial variation of out-of-town centres: their distribution is weakest in areas such as Southern England where Conservative political strength is greatest.

5.2 THE PLANNING PROCESS

The resistance to out-of-town shopping centres is easily promoted because two of the three protagonists are intimately involved in the planning process, whilst the third is usually there by virtue of double role playing.

The first part of the processing of the application involves the expertise of a local council's professional staff, who are responsible for assessing the accuracy of the information contained in a planning application, seeing that the application complies with the law and giving a judgment on the overall merits of the proposal. In terms of the accuracy of the information it is not uncommon for the developer, or his representatives, and the professional staff to get together beforehand to see that there are no glaring discrepancies in the factual information: it is obviously in the interests of the former rather than the latter to do so. In one of the out-of-town centre proposals near Colchester, for example,

---

[1] This is a very common practice in North America, for example, where rural local authorities are appreciative of the extra rateable value. In order to tap the urban market and compete with existing centres it is not uncommon to find the out-of-town centre adjacent to the local authority boundary along some arterial route. It is also common to find planning regulations more favourable for shopping centre development on the rural side of the boundary. Such development could eventually pave the way for annexation by the urban area.

both sides had early on agreed to facts relating to vehicle movements, road capacity, the anticipated turnover of the centre and the impact on the convenience-food trade within 10 and 15 minute driving times of the centre (Department of the Environment, 1977b). Again from the point of view of complying with the law, it is in the interests of the developer, given the slow legal process anyway, to see that the application is properly presented either by doing the necessary legal work beforehand or seeking the advice of the local authority's own legal staff.

However, in giving a judgment on the merits of a proposal the local authority's professional staff can place a very different interpretation on the same material compared to the developer's staff and consultants. Also, the former is likely to consider the proposal in a wider context than simply the retail implications and thus have a more comprehensive case should the proposal be recommended for rejection. Much of the relevant information in a planning application is of necessity qualitative, and therefore the interpretation by both sides could differ considerably; for example, the amount of extra vehicular traffic before the loss of amenity becomes unacceptable (unacceptable to whom?). But quantitative information is also open to dispute in the way it is interpreted. The developer and professional staff agreed on the impact of the Sainsbury's superstore near Colchester which was a 8.7 per cent loss of trade from the stores within the 10 minute driving time and 7.1 per cent within 15 minutes (Department of the Environment, 1977b). The developer found this acceptable, but the professional staff chose to argue that these losses would prejudice both existing retail facilities and any expansions, currently under consideration or approved, once these were developed.[1]

The second part of the planning approval process, running concurrently and/or subsequently, involves the consideration of the application by the local authority's planning committee; this consists of elected representatives and their staff advisors. Having received their officers' recommendations and public comment, they may suggest areas for further study and often make recommendations for acceptance or rejection to the full council. Since this is the committee with the greatest political clout, especially if full council is essentially a rubber stamp organisation, it is likely to be the area where the most intense lobbying activity will take place: this includes not only those for or against the out-of-town centre proposal, but also professional staff with their knowledge of the intricacies of planning matters and their informal and unwritten role of educating the local politician. Some much so that local politicians may be quite

---

[1] It was not stated how existing and proposed retail facilities would be prejudiced from the point of view of possible individual store turnover losses and closures, nor whether any of the proposed facilities themselves might not be just as guilty in prejudicing those already in existence.

content merely to endorse a staff recommendation, all the more so if the former are relatively new to council or the sentiments of the recommendation are similar to those expressed by the small businessman. It is often hard for the developer to compete, given the better access that the small businessman and professional staff have to the local politician. One approach, adopted by Sainsbury's in the Colchester example, was to invite the planning committee to view a similar development, in this case Sainsbury's Cherry Hinton superstore near Cambridge, in order to assuage the fears concerning the detrimental effects of out-of-town centres. It would seem that the planning committee was not convinced since the application was eventually rejected. Indeed, for many local politicians, who hitherto had not experienced out-of-town shopping centres, a visit such as this could have persuaded them that this type of shopping was not desireable.

This part of the approval stage brings an added complication. Politicians can be both the jury and the counsel for the prosecution, since they are required to pass judgment on the merits of a particular planning application, yet beforehand may have been seen to be in a majority against the application for various reasons. This is not a situation that applies merely to the consideration of out-of-town shopping centres. Politicians are constantly required to make decisions in the public interest against a background of their perception of what is in the public interest; this perception in turn may be affected by personal bias resulting out of some degree of involvement in the subject area. As seen above, in the case of out-of-town centres this involvement may arise through local politicians being at the same time small businessmen; and even if not, politicians can be in support of other facets of the retail sector which they may feel will be unduly threatened should the out-of-town centre be built.

The third stage of the planning approval process involves the central government, presently through the Secretary of State for the Environment. This, however, is not mandatory procedure and is only invoked should one or other of two conditions apply. First, if a local planning authority refuses an application for planning permission or unnecessarily delays in making a decision, the applicant has the right to a planning inquiry before an inspector appointed by the Secretary of State; and on hearing the evidence the inspector may recommend to the Secretary of State that the application be approved or rejected. Second, the Secretary of State, on the advice of Department of the Environment officials, may call in a planning application for consideration and possibly public inquiry, irrespective of a local planning authority's opinion or decision. This situation can arise if the proposal for an out-of-town centre is deemed to be a major divergence from approved Development Plans or Structure/Local Plans, involves more than one local authority, is beyond the ability of a local authority to handle the situation (this is perhaps less true since local government reorganisation in the mid 1970s) or more than one application is involved (e.g. Cribbs Causeway, near Bristol, and Colchester). A further criterion

for possible call-in is the size of the centre. It was first
asked that the Secretary of State be informed by local
authorities of all applications for out-of-town centres over
50 000 sq.ft. (gross space) (Department of the Environment,
1972c).[1] In 1976 this figure was amended to read 100 000 sq.
ft., on the basis that sufficient information was known about
the effects of smaller out-of-town centres for local authorities
to be able to process applications unaided.

The planning inquiry procedure takes the out-of-town shopping
debate out of the local political arena and may eliminate many
of the biases that have been seen. However, only a minority
of planning applications that are refused ever get to the
inquiry stage. Many planning applications are variations of
other applications, some of which are submitted by the same
developer for the same site at the same time, and intended to
elicit local planning authority preference (if any!). A
developer may realise, on the basis of the type of opposition
generated and the reason for refusal, that the application
stands so little chance of being approved that it is not worth
the legal costs involved of taking it to a planning inquiry.
Finally, a developer may in some way change his intentions,
e.g. submit a new application, or withdraw from shopping
centre development altogether.

Those applications which go before a planning inquiry are
dealt with in a far from consistent fashion. Lee and Kent
(1976) state that the burden of proof still rests with the
shopping centre developer; but there is little possibility in
using a formal planning policy on out-of-town centres as a
yardstick since inspectors have scant regard for this (it may
be because such a policy is hard to discern!) and tend to
resolve issues pragmatically, judging each case on its own
merits. A major consideration amongst inspectors is in fact
land use and protection of the countryside; but an examination
of planning inquiry materials reveals that, unless the site
is a 'green field' location, what is meant by protection of
the countryside can vary tremendously. Similarly, inspectors
have no objection to causing more competition amongst retailers
but have no wish to undermine an established centre or shopping
hierarchy. However, the means by which inspectors judge
whether an out-of-town centre will damage the existing retail
structure rather than complement it are often inadequate and
open to the same differences in interpretation as seen above
in the Sainsbury's versus Colchester Council example.

Whilst the biases of the local politician or professional
planner cannot interefere with an inspector's decision, it
can be seen that the planning inquiry is in some ways merely
an extension of the local planning machinery. The emphasis
is still on development control rather than viewing out-of-

---

[1] Establishing a 50 000 sq.ft. figure was an invitation for
developers to submit proposals which did not exceed this
figure!

town centres as an acceptable (or unacceptable) innovation on policy grounds and therefore plan (or not plan) for them accordingly. The planning inquiry requires an inspector to adjudicate in what is a dispute over the use of a piece of land. In terms of the wider issues and ramifications in the shopping centre debate, inspectors are required to be selective. They are not asked to look at (although some do it of their own accord) such issues as should out-of-town shopping centres be allowed, what alternate locations are suitable, and will consumers benefit from the new shopping facilities, issues which might be described as innovative policy areas. On the other hand, it is very much Ministerial policy (and a great deal of attention is paid at planning inquiries) to look into the effect of out-of-town centres on existing land use and policy relating to the present retail structure and various aspects of urban and rural amenity. However, planning inquiries into Structure Plans have shown that it is possible to examine policy rather than land use and to be innovative rather than extend the status quo.

The pragmatic, each case on its own merits, approach to a planning inquiry results of course in considerable uncertainty as to whether an inspector will recommend to the Secretary of State that a planning application be approved or rejected. There is a better than two to one chance, based on previous experience, that a planning application refused by a local authority will also be turned down by a planning inspector. Given the limitations that are placed on planning inspectors (or the limitations they place on themselves), there is little doubt that they act in as fair manner as possible in hearing witnesses and receiving evidence from assessors in matters where inspectors may not feel competent or a second independent opinion would be valuable. However, it would be rash to suggest that inspectors do not hold an opinion for or against out-of-town centres, and that the course of an inquiry will not be so affected. There is certainly a gut reaction in both the development industry and amongst local authorities that a recommendation for acceptance (or rejection) is more likely from one inspector compared to another.

The final stage in the planning process involves the receiving of the inspector's recommendations by the Secretary of State for the Environment (or rather officials of that Department) for further consideration and eventual Ministerial decision. Lee and Kent (1976) argue that the time lapse is considerable where planning permission has been granted, the outstanding example being two and a half years in the Cribbs Causeway case. Such consideration may seem unnecessary in the light of the overwhelming majority of recommendations being endorsed by the Secretary of State. It is, however, an opportunity for further judgment on the various issues and conflicting opinions, although it should be added that some of this may be carried out by career civil servants with perhaps little expertise in the fields involved. The result is that the Secretary of State in his decision letter may endorse or change the inspector's recommendations. In the Asda superstore proposal at Great Yarmouth, for example, the Secretary of State disagreed with the inspector on the question of industrial land and

stated that it was unwise to use it for other purposes
(Department of the Environment, 1972d). Irrespective of the
inspector's recommendation both the developer and the local
authority are given a breathing space somehow to persuade
the Minister and his officials to see a certain point of view.
A final aspect of this period of consideration is the
opportunity to solicit impartial advice from other government
ministries which may or may not have been contacted earlier:
it must be recognised that earlier contact at the local
planning approval stage may have been with the intent of
supporting a particular stand for or against an out-of-town
centre. In instances where the Secretary of State has
overturned an inspector's recommendation, it has usually been
to refuse an earlier call for granting planning permission.
In the Sainsbury's superstore proposal near Colchester, for
example, the Secretary of State in refusing planning permission
questioned the inspector's conclusion that the store would
have little effect on the town centre; he concluded that
given new floorspace (completed or proposed) in the town centre
as well as converted warehouse accommodation in the same
general area as the superstore, there is less need for the
new development. Moreover, he lends support to the prematurity
argument, that it would be preferable to wait until a policy
on future shopping patterns is submitted as part of the Essex
Structure Plan (Department of the Environment, 1977b).

A final, yet rarely instituted, part of the planning process
is to appeal against a Secretary of State's decision before
the High Court on the basis that he acted in contravention of
the Town and Country Planning Act. One case was that involving
J. Sainsbury Ltd. v. Secretary of State for the Environment
and Colchester Borough Council (1978). The Applicants felt
that the Secretary of State erred in his judgment by referring
to matters not brought before the public inquiry and therefore
a new public inquiry should be held. Mr Graham Eyre, Q.C.,
who sat as the deputy judge, concluded that the Secretary of
State acted responsibly, and in disagreeing with the inspector
and refusing planning permission did so on the basis of only
a different interpretation of the same statement of facts.
It was felt that there were no grounds for interfering with
the Secretary of State's decision.

It can be seen that a planning process which reflects mostly
opposition at a local level is matched by one of extreme
caution at a higher level, should the local refusal be
appealed in the first place or the proposal called in. The
emphases on development control, judging each case on its own
merits and being selective in the wider issues that government
wishes to take into account have been major deterrents in the
spread of out-of-town centres in Britain compared to North
America and other parts of Europe.

5.3 THE NATURE OF RESISTANCE TO CHANGE

Once the groups opposing out-of-town centres have been
identified and attention is given to the planning process
which enables this opposition to find an outlet, it is
important to consider the nature of the resistance, the

factors underlying it and the extent to which this resistance
features in the decision-making process. It was earlier
mentioned that there is a good deal of selectivity in the
wider issues that are taken into account in the shopping
centre debate: the issues which are frequently considered
are all too often those in which opponents of out-of-town
centres are seen to be prominent. The resistance to out-of-
town shopping centres from a retail point of view focusses
on two major arguments. First, that the existing shopping
facilities and those already approved or proposed within the
traditional retail hierarchy will adequately take care of the
needs of the population in the foreseeable future. Second,
and in a sense following from it, to approve large increases
in space at an out-of-town centre could only have damaging
effects on existing shopping facilities. These are the
problems that one will find expanded upon at most local
planning committee meetings and planning inquiries, and
justification is sought, and easily found, to support these
two arguments on various social and economic grounds. However,
there are a number of other implications involved, which are
all too often masked since they do not present logical planning
arguments. Resistance is frequently the result of fear, real
or imagined, that the out-of-town centre will upset the status
quo in which an individual or group has a particular vested
interest. The following identify the major areas of
resistance:

The protection of the small retailer One of the most
vociferous groups against out-of-town centres has been the
small, independent retailer acting usually through local
Chambers of Trade. Whilst the general arguments they put
forward against such centres may seen quite reasonable in
planning terms, it must be remembered that they do so not
just in the wider community interest but also from the point
of view of protecting their own livelihoods. Most, if not
all, out-of-town centre proposals have been met with some
form of opposition from this quarter and others (local
politicians, for example) acting on its behalf. But very
often the grounds for the opposition are exceedingly misplaced
In spite of the very extensive impact studies that have been
undertaken (see Chapter 3), and even allowing for the problems
associated with them, it is clear that the results of all this
work have not filtered well through the system and there is a
good deal of ignorance and misplaced hostility at the local
level concerning the effects of an out-of-town centre.
Furthermore, there is evidence of less than reasonable
behaviour.

First, an out-of-town centre proposal is too readily greeted
by most small shopkeepers as being disastrous to existing
trade, without taking into account the location of the centre,
its size, its convenience-durable goods ratio and of course,
the other on-going processes which could be affecting existing
trade. It is likely that an out-of-twn centre could affect
all trade in existing centres to some degree by syphoning off
some consumers permanently. Not that these consumers will be
satisfied entirely by the out-of-town centre, but they will
combine shopping here with visits to other different centres.

Except in a few circumstances noted in Chapter 3, it is highly unlikely that the effect will be disastrous, and if so, it is likely to be confined to certain types of convenience -good stores (often not involving the small, independent retailer!). It seems faintly ludicrous to see the specialty durable-goods store owner fearing that an out-of-town centre will put him out of business. Yet it is this type of store owner who is so prominent in local chambers of trade and who will work so fervently to see an out-of-town centre proposal defeated.

Second, in order to protect their interests against encroachment the small retailer may resort to various tactics to convince the decision-making body. They often speak in the wider community interest (protecting the rateable value of existing centres, for example) or support positions in which they have little direct interest, such as the amenity value of a particular rural area. Also, they will refer government to the effects of out-of-town centres. However, unlike developers and local authorities who have the resources to do their own assessment of likely impact, chambers of trade tend to draw upon experiences in other areas to back up their arguments. It is probably both the result of stabbing in the dark and finding the evidence that will highlight their cause, that the analogies drawn upon sometimes fall short of the mark. The much publicised report of the Carrefour hyper-market at Caerphilly (Lee and Kent, 1975) is used for this purpose, perhaps because it shows some rather dramatic effects in terms of shop closures in the Caerphilly town centre and therefore would create the right impression when trying to plant the same idea elsewhere. The Colchester and District Chamber of Trade and Commerce used this evidence, admittedly scaled down, when opposing the Sainsbury's superstore (Department of the Environment, 1977b). However, Colchester is not Caerphilly, and the developer's own studies agreed to by the local planning authority, showed a markedly lower level of impact.

Third, the small retailer is expecting government to protect him from any competition (or rather any further competition) in the system. Often this type of competition is labelled as unfair, although it is difficult to see just what is thought of as fair and unfair competition. The latter perhaps refers to the fact that the small retailer is excluded from the out-of-town centre and thus cannot take advantage of the benefits of the location. (And thus, if he cannot take advantage, then by implication no one else, e.g. large companies and the consumer, should either). Also, the degree of fairness may relate directly to the size of the centre and its likely impact. However, this type of protectionism, and using the decision-making body to support it (even if indirectly), flies in the face of traditional concepts and attitudes adopted by the businessman, including the notions of free enterprise and competition and the dislike of government intervention in the economy. Moreover, any form of protectionism heightens inefficiencies in the system which are reflected eventually in higher than necessary economic and social costs to the public.

Fourth, resistance to the out-of-town centre is seen as yet
another attempt to close the stable door, and hopefully this
time not after the horse has bolted.   It has been shown in
Chapter 2 that retailing has been undergoing considerable
change in its institutional arrangements since the Second
World War as a larger share of the market has been taken
over by regional and national multiple-store firms.   The
small retailer is often powerless to do anything about it:
he is often not aware of what is going on until it is too
late, the multiples move into existing premises in town and
district centres, thereby requiring no change of use
permission, and where they are part of redevelopment schemes
they have received local and central government sanction.
However, the small retailer can at least stem the loss of
trade to the multiples by the spin-off effect of being in
the same retail centres and being visible to the same
consumers.   The out-of-town centre phenomenon is part of the
same process of multiple firm expansion, intra-industry
competition and rationalisation.   But the choice of new
locations and lack of spin-off effects to the small retailer
have understandably raised his ire, and through the planning
and development control mechanism this group has found a way
to lobby against such retail developments.

Finally, there is little real understanding by the small
retailer that consumers may actually prefer out-of-town
shopping facilities and therefore should be given an
opportunity to satisfy this preference.   The success of
existing out-of-town centres and the lengths to which the
small retailer will go in opposing any new proposals suggest
that the consumer's preference is being understood.   But the
tendency is to excuse the consumer in a patronising way,
saying they are influenced by high pressure sales tactics,
heavy advertising, cut prices, free car parking and so on.
These are presumably the unfair practices, since the small
retailer feels unable to compete.   The small retailer has
yet to accept fully the suburbanisation of non-convenience
retail facilities and to play an active role along with local
authorities and/or multiple firms in the establishment of
out-of-town and district centres.

The protection of the existing retail hierarchy   All three
identified in 5.1 have a special interest in promoting, and
therefore protecting, the existing retail hierarchy;   they
have been responsible for its recent development in terms of
planning, implementation and the investment of public and
private monies.   In the intra-urban context, as shown in 2.6,
a four-level hierarchy of town, district and neighbourhood
centres and smaller shopping parades/corner stores has evolved
over the last century, reflecting various aspects of retail
and consumer behaviour.   More recently, this hierarchy has
been embodied in Development Plans at the local level, although
the actual hierarchy seen in any area is constantly undergoing
change;   older shopping areas in the inner city have frequently
declined because of population movement and urban renewal
whilst newer suburban areas have attracted their own
neighbourhood shopping facilities.

Local politicians and professional staff have also been involved with the changes that have been taking place. In both private and council housing areas land use plans to be approved by a local council are accompanied by details of the area to be set aside for shopping facilities. At the outline planning stage there may be no information on the type of store mix, but it will be noted whether the total acreage set aside is appropriate for the necessary store types, parking etc., given the size of the new population and other shopping facilities in the area. Determining the store mix can only effectively be done if the local council owns the shops; however, this is frequently not a problem since much of the shopping development, even on private estates, is undertaken by the local council with the shops (and the flats above) then rented out. The vast majority of these developments have been in the neighbourhood centre type and are duplicated across a suburban area with monotonous regularity. In a few instances local councils have encouraged district centres, for example, Cowley in Oxford, allowing for more competitive convenience functions and the inclusion of some durable goods, thereby hoping to relieve pressure on town centres. In addition to shopping, local councils have been financially involved in a wide range of activities which are necessary to make local shopping viable, including housing provision and/or approval, public utilities, roads and bus transportation.

A more visable and impressive record of local government involvement in shopping has been in the historic town centres across Britain, although this is part of a Comprehensive Development Area scheme concerning other commercial land uses, public buildings and institutions, housing, open space, roads and car parking (see, for example, Guy, 1980). This involvement largely dates from the Second World War and was a response to the serious destruction of many town centres through enemy action. There was an immediate need in some cities to provide outlets where people could do their shopping. Also, the large cleared areas where shops and offices had once stood were seen as an opportunity to provide a better town centre environment, including a functionally improved shopping and office area, better roads and a more aesthetically pleasing use of open space and design of building. Gradually, over the next thirty years the programme has been expanded to eradicate the worst legacies of the nineteenth century (or earlier), and to accommodate the needs of today's shoppers, office workers and so on. Few cities over 50 000 people have not undertaken some form of comprehensive development, and the vastness of the programme is a result of central government, as well as local government, involvement. Many local schemes, even allowing for the bare mimimum of change that was necessary, were beyond the resources of local rates and could have only succeded with heavy subsidy from central government. Moreover, central government provided the mechanism to implement this type of change, for example, land assembly. However, given the legal and financial support of central government, local government has engaged in a programme that is generally far from the bare minimum! In order to accommodate people's needs (or supposed needs) there has often been the wholesale destruction of very

sound buildings (even historic buildings), so much so that
Victoria architecture once so abundant is now seriously
threatened. Many core areas that were surrounded by slums,
industry, warehouses and lines of straggling shops now find
themselves surrounded (and separated from inner city
residential areas) by a great swath of land for improved
roads, surface and multi-storey car parking and institutional
uses. Meanwhile the core area often has limited vehicular
access, pedestrian and delivery vehicle only streets and
the development of off-street shopping precincts or single
or multi-level covered shopping malls.

Town centre redevelopment in Britain would not have been
possible without the financial support of the private sector.
But given the generous level of government support it has
perhaps been cheaper to develop in the town centre rather
than bear a far larger proportion of the total cost of an
out-of-town location. Over the years most of the major
property development companies in the non-residential field
and major multiple retailers have been concerned with town
centre redevelopment and have established working relationships
with central and local government. Frequently, it can be said
to be too good a relationship, which can be seen in the way
local government is prepared to compromise publically owned
land and buildings and the life styles of its citizenry in
order to bend to the wishes of the private sector and not lose
(to some nearby town perhaps) a massive infusion of private
capital.

The development of the out-of-town centre is seen as a major
challenge to the retail hierarchy at all levels. However,
unlike existing centres, there is little or no loyalty amongst
professional staff and local politicians to aid in their
promotion. The local planning authority's opposition (and
that of neighbouring authorities) may focus on whether the
out-of-town is in the community interest, but it must be
remembered that part of this community interest is the
protection of the public's investment in rival retail centres.

The town centre represents to local politicians and professional
staff the area which would stand to lose the most through out-
of-town centre development, since it is in some towns the only
major comparison goods centre and also perhaps the only major
supermarket shopping area. Furthermore, a decline in the
retail sector would spark an increase in store vacancies, a
decline in investment by the private sector, a deteriorating
physical environment and spin-off effects perhaps in other
areas of the town centre economy, resulting in an overall
loss of confidence. An analogy is frequently drawn here,
albeit only half correctly, with the situation in North
American cities over the last thirty years.

In the British context the out-of-town centre is viewed as a
threat to changes in progress in nearby town centres. These
changes are considered to be sufficiently great in terms of
their upheaval and need for readjustment that the last thing
a town wants is a further period of uncertainty. At present
many town centres are attempting to adapt to increasing car

useage, an improved shopping environment (off-street precincts and covered malls) and technological changes in the retail industry (larger supermarkets or superstores). The result is that many of the things that could happen should an out-of-town centre be built are in fact happening: for example, a large, new, town centre shopping precinct without a matching demolition of older shops can result in an overprovision of shopping facilities, a large number of vacancies (in both old and new stores) and a bleak, ill-kept appearance, especially if the vacancies are concentrated, and an invitation perhaps to vandalism and loss of consumer confidence in the area. A major factor behind the local authority's rejection of superstores and hypermarkets in the Colchester area was that the town centre had seen a 30 per cent increase in its retail space between 1971 and 1976 which in its wake had created at one time as many as 65 unoccupied older shops, representing over 7 per cent of the total retail outlets in the town centre (Department of the Environment, 1977b). In effect, the local authority was arguing that having already created an overprovision of retail space it did not wish to compound the problem.

It is probably more true to say that local authorities are applying two different codes of behaviour: whilst it is acceptable to allow for overprovision in existing centres (or, more likely, justify it when it happens since the scenario was probably not foreseen), the same is not to be accepted when it would benefit solely a private developer and multiple firm(s) in an out-of-town centre. Furthermore, knowingly allowing for overprovision can be seen in the inconsistent, even hypocritical, behaviour engaged in by local authorities. To reject an out-of-town centre on the basis of no need for increased floor space given existing and already approved retail facilities elsewhere is logical. But at the same time this argument is being used many local authorities are giving permission for increased floorspace in existing retail centres, very often the same type of floorspace - just a different, but more preferred, location. The Colchester example readily shows this inconsistency. At the same time as the Secretary of State for the Environment was considering the planning inspectors' reports for the Sainsbury's, Asda and Carrefour superstore proposals on the western edge of Colchester at Stanway (all of which the local authority had refused), planning permission was given to Tesco (which had also been refused permission for an out-of-town development) to build a 60 000 sq.ft. superstore along with a publically financed multi-storey car park in the town centre.

The inconsistency in the resistance to out-of-town centres and the promotion of the status quo go beyond just floorspace. The local planning authority argued against the superstore and hypermarket proposals on the western edge of Colchester on the grounds that a district centre in the area already provided fairly adequate shopping provision. However, the district centre constitutes an industrial estate, the stores are converted warehouses, car parking (5.4 spaces per 1 000 sq.ft) and approach roads are woefully inadequate, and conflict exists between industrial and shopping traffic; these are

83

hardly the right bases on which to promote a district centre. Second, a further reason for rejection was the amount of traffic and resulting noise, fumes, unpleasantness and hazardous crossings along the main road to the west of Colchester (formerly the A12 trunk route) and a policy by the local council to restrict shopping provision as much as possible: it was on this same road (and at a key junction) that Sainsbury's were later given permission to build a smaller supermarket!

The promotion of town centre redevelopment and opposition to out-of-town centres may be done with the intent of protecting public investment, providing the consumer with a wide variety of shopping opportunities and enhancing the image and historic position of a town, but the cost involved in taking this particular stance is rarely considered to the same degree, nor are comparative costs taken into account. The development industry is very cognisant of the cheaper land and building costs in an out-of-town (or even district centre) location and many studies have been done on relative costs, but the same concern fails to enter the public domain. Moreover, there is less realisation than there should be concerning the problems and costs which result from concentrating retail development in the town centre. The chief problem here is one of circulation and car parking. Had car-ownership levels in Britain stayed at early 1950s levels then a more positive case could be made for retail development on such a grand scale in the town centre. But rising car ownership levels over the years, the preference of consumers for car useage (even where an adequate bus service exists) and technological and institutional changes in the retail industry which encourage car useage (e.g. weekly bulk grocery purchasing) have put untold pressures on town centres in terms of needing better access routes and car-parking facilities which eventually have had to be provided at considerable public cost. If greater consideration had been given to justifying those costs, in terms of whether cheaper alternatives were available, and if this had been required by central government, then a stronger argument would have existed for out-of-town shopping centre locations. Better access routes and car-parking and pedestrianisation have been seen too readily as a means of improving the town centre rather than the expensiv results of a policy of overtly concentrating both convenience and comparison-good items in the one, traditionally congested perhaps, location.

The planning inquiries into the Colchester superstore and hypermarket proposals, for example, are mute testament to the fact that in opposing one kind of retail development there will be wider repercussions in other parts of the retail hierarchy (Department of the Environment, 1977b). The developers refer to the poor state of car-parking provision in the Colchester town centre; this amounted to 2.19 spaces per 1 000 sq.ft. gross floor space, whereas a government sponsored study recommends 5.75 spaces for central shopping areas of sub-regional centres (National Economic Development Office, 1971). Whilst this ratio has improved as more multi-storey car parking was provided, the benefits will not be realised if retail space is expanded too. (This situation did happen and was further exacerbated by financial and timing restrictings being placed on more car parking). Furthermore, the developers did nor raise the costly need to complete the town centre ring road system. The local authority on the other hand, spent hours of testimony on out-of-town centre traffic problems and made little or no mention of the problems endured at that time by the town centre or likely to be created once approved plans were completed. It was argued by the local authority that the Colchester town centre was not any less attractive for shoppers in 1976 than in 1971, in spite of the 30 per cent increase in retail floor space. This could be claimed to be a less than honest statement, otherwise why was so much attention being given to improving car parking. Besides, one is hardly being facetious when suggesting that the town centre remains attractive since for some there are no convenient alternatives: Colchester, like many other towns, has a dismal record of district centre provision, let alone out-of-town centres, and as a result it does lose trade to other centres where car useage is easier.

5.4   CONCLUSION

Out of town shopping centre proposals from the private sector have met with resistance not from the consumer but from groups who have either a professional, political or business interest in promoting, and thus protecting, the status quo. Professional groups have generally steered clear of making pronouncements for or against, instead leaving it to invididuals working for government to judge (and invariably oppose) as they (or their employers) see fit. The chief opposition has centred around the small retailer and the local politician, both of whom, when not realising perhaps the actual impact of an out-of-town centre, are panicked into opposition in order to protect the traditional retail hierarchy and changes already taking place within it. The planning process has made it easy for local opposition to defeat out-of-town centre proposals, including the emphasis on development control, the possible dual role of government as judge and opponent and the inconsistency of the wider issues that are considered.

6. Government policy and planning and retail innovation

The small number of out-of-town shopping centres in Britain and the resistance towards these by various groups are a reflection of both government policies in the retail sector as a whole and its 'policy of no policy' on out-of-town centres in particular. Whilst government involvement in the British economy has increased tremendously over the years, it can be seen that the retail sector is one of the exceptions; and where there has been government involvement, it has tended to be diffused amongst a number of central government departments and or given over to local government to decide (with the central government acting as an adjudicator should a dispute arise in the planning process or local decisions conflict with central government policy). Given the nature and strengths of the retail hierarchy that have developed over time and government actions in allied areas (e.g. central city redevelopment schemes), the tendency has been for government policy and planning approval in the retail sector to favour the status quo or err on the side of caution should any retail innovation be proposed. So much of what happens in the retail sector has taken place in fact with little or no government involvement simply because the industry has not sought government financial help or does not contravene any law or regulation. However, the out-of-town shopping centre phenomenon is one in which both central and local governments are intimately involved: planning permission is needed under the Town and Country Planning Act (as shown in 5.2) and the full force of government policy, or lack of policy, comes into effect at this time.

This chapter will examine the nature of government policies towards both the retail sector as a whole and the out-of-town shopping centre which are undertaken at the various governmental levels, including national (central), sub-regional and county/district. Attention will be paid first to the information inputs upon which policy formulation is frequently based.

6.1 RETAIL INFORMATION

In the last twenty years there has been extensive research undertaken in the industrialised countries, in both the private sector and the universities, on many facets of retailing and consumer behaviour; and it is possible from this to observe very definite trends in terms of retail and consumer change on which to formulate policy and plan for change in both the short and long term (see for example Davies, 1976; Dawson, 1979; 1980; Guy, 1980). In the British context, however, there has been a regrettable lack of foresight on the part of government in utilising this information. Second, the central government has been lax in filling the voids in the information by conducting their own studies, especially in areas beyond the scope and financial resources of the private and university sectors, such as the monitoring of national trends. To some extent this is a reflection of the lack of central government interest in so many aspects of retailing and the feeling that it is the responsibility of private industry, normal market forces involving the consumer and the regulatory procedures imposed by the local authority.

It was not until the late 1960s, after nearly two decades of considerable readjustments in the retail sector, many of which were causing serious pressures in the system, that government became more involved in the information seeking process. However, even then, the initiatives came as much from quasi-public bodies, such as the Economic Development Office for the Distributive Trades in N.E.D.O. (National Economic Development Office) as from the central government ministries directly. The former had mainly a research and policy suggestion role and was frequently critical of the government's actions, or lack of actions, in the retail area. In some instances the Economic Development Committee carried out work on behalf of government and aided both in policy formulation and planning for retail change and justifying policies which had already been adopted.

One of the earliest influential studies was that undertaken by the Economic Development Committee for the Distributive Trades on the Cowley Shopping Centre in Oxford (N.E.D.O., 1968). Whilst the study was the result of an interest in problems of investment and shopping capacity, an important by-product was the role played by a suburban district centre, built by the local authority, in providing new forms of retail development, relieving town centre congestion and providing consumers with greater convenience. Furthermore, it was possible to gauge the likely impact of future developments. The interest of the government in this type of retail development, and thus this study, can be seen from the fact that the Ministry of Housing and Local Government was engaged at the same time in studying the development of district centres (Ministry of Housing and Local Government, 1969). It was recognised that far reaching changes were occurring in the retail sector because of rising car ownership and developments in the retail trade itself, and the study aimed at anticipating the kind of shopping centre distribution within towns and loosely structured urban regions that would most likely meet the needs of consumers and retailers in the future.

In spite of government interest and support for promoting district centres, it was argued by the Economic Development Committee for the Distributive Trades that the government was only in a limited way interested in the retail questions (National Economic Development Office, 1971). The Secretary of State for the Environment was concerned with the amount and location of retail floorspace in Comprehensive Development Areas and new towns; but elsewhere unless there was an appeal against a local authority refusal or an application was called in, the Secretary of State was only concerned with broad land use and planning issues or operating in an advisory capacity. Moreover, whilst there were various interest groups, including government departments, who were keen to know more about the future shape and size of shopping capacity, there was no umbrella organisation to do this work. There was a very real fear, for example, that there may be overprovision of retail facilities in some areas and a lack of adequate facilities in other areas.

A Shopping Capacity Sub-Committee was set up by the Economic Development Committee to attempt to alleviate these problems by advising on   i) the work being carried out elsewhere; ii) the pattern and capacity likely in ten to twenty years assuming unchanged legislation, past trends and experiences in other countries;   iii) which pattern capacity made the best use of resources, economic efficiency and greatest consumer convenience;   and iv) the implications all this would have for urban physical and economic planning policies. The ensuing study found that excess capacity was highly likely given current trends continuing and the requirements based on consumer expenditures (N.E.D.O., 1971). The actual number of shops would continue to decline, whilst multiple stores would increase their share of the total market at the expense of independent retailers. Rationalisation would result in ever larger supermarkets (superstores), run by a few large chains, accounting for an increased proportion of total food sales. The Sub-Committee recognised that car travel would increase significantly, although less frequent shopping trips would be made. Finally, town centres would retail approximately the same proportion of trade while planned district and neighbourhood centres would take an increasing proportion of trade at the expense of marginal parades and street corner activities. Given the current climate it saw no major increase in free-standing, out-of-town stores and centres, although it suggested that there were many advantages in developing this type of facility as well as the favourable response amongst consumers. The Sub-Committee stated that the argument that town centres should be preserved was an assertion rather than a fact, since little in the way of any cost-benefit analysis had ever taken place.

The Sub-Committee made a number of recommendations. The most important in this context were first that there was a clear need for a regional strategy, given the hierarchical structure of retail activity, the inadequacies of local government at the time and the clear indications of overprovision of retail facilities. It was hoped that changes to the Town and Country Planning Act in 1968 (and again in 1971), which set out the formulation of structure and local planning, and the possible reorganisation of local government (finally achieved in 1974) would help in this regard. Second, there was a need for a co-ordinating body, under a government department, a university or a separate institute, to look at shopping provision and change on an ongoing basis and to use more disaggregated data.[1] Third, it was recommended that although the members of the Sub-Committee were divided on their opinions towards free-standing stores and centres, the Department of the Environment should lay down guidelines on the criteria for their acceptability.[2]

During the 1970s the development industry, retailers and policymakers have been aided by a plethora of retail studies (see Thorpe, 1978a, table 2; and 3.1 above); whilst these largely relate to out-of-town superstores and centres, it is possible to gauge what is happening to existing centres. Furthermore, extensive retail information has been gathered in the course of academic study, structure and local plan formulation and conducting appeals into local authority planning refusals. However, the outcome of all this work has to be viewed in part as local and piecemeal, and there is a need for more comprehensive study, acting as a follow up to that done by the Shopping Capacity Sub-Committee (N.E.D.O., 1971).

It must be recognised, on the other hand, that more and better information does not necessarily lead to better or more realistic policy-making on the part of government. It can be noted that the information that we do have has only been partially successful, for example, in lessening the hostility of government towards out-of-town centres; thereby exemplifying that policy may be based more on emotions, misconceptions or priorities in non-retail areas rather than information relating strictly to retailing.

6.2 NATIONAL (CENTRAL) GOVERNMENT POLICY

The key to the success of out-of-town centres in Britain ultimately rests with central government and more specifically the Department of the Environment. But the approach that government has adopted over the years is similar to that in other parts of the retail sector which includes limited and

---

[1] The Unit for Retail Planning Information Ltd. was subsequently set up in Reading and is funded jointly by the private and public sector to undertake retail studies. However, this organisation is relatively small, and in fact more work is still undertaken by other groups, including the Department of the Environment, the Retail Outlets Research Unit at the Manchester Business School (see Thorpe, 1978b) and private consultants and academics.

[2] This was done the following year (see Department of the Environment, 1972c). A critique of these guidelines will be seen in 6.2.

diffused involvement and often ambiguous guidelines (to
retailers and local authorities) rather than concrete policy
and directives (Davies, 1977).

First of all a number of government departments with widely
diverging responsibilities have an influence in the retail
sector, including, besides the Department of the Environment,
those departments concerned with Trade and Industry,
Employment, Transport, Agriculture and Food, Health and the
Treasury. Even within the one department, such as the
Environment, there can be disparate views, for example between
those concerned with green belt and rural land use policies
(and the effect retailing has on these) and others whose
concern in strictly the provision of more adequate retail
opportunities.

This limited and diffused involvement follows from the low
priority placed on the retail sector from the central
government's point of view. Before the Second World War
retailing was almost entirely the responsibility of the
entrepreneur with government, or local government, intervening
principally in areas relating to standards (opening hours,
weights and measures, food quality, building codes, etc.)
and the taxation of property and goods. It was largely with
the approval of the Town and Country Planning Act, 1947 that
the government first became involved in any overall sense
with the land use planning, control and approval of retail
uses; although Mills (1974) and others have noted that the
1947 Act in fact says very little about retail activity,
leaving it to local authorities to report on their own retail
land uses and proposals for future developments. As mentioned
earlier, by the 1940s a very well established hierarchical
pattern of shopping centres existed in both the inter- and
intra-urban context, and central government policy and action
subsequently tended to endorse this (e.g. the major investments
in town centre redevelopment). The same emphasis on the
retail hierarchy has permeated new residential development
such as the New and Expanded Town programme and major suburban
expansions in both the public and private sector. The central
government was not directly involved in the planning and
implementation of many of these new centres; but it often
acted in an advisory capacity or provided financial resources
and in these ways it was possible for traditional concepts in
shopping centre location to be promoted or encouraged.

In the 1960s the Ministry of Housing and Local Government
(the Department of the Environment's predecessor) faced
increasing criticism both internally and from retailers and
local authorities concerning the overemphasis on promoting
town centre development and redevelopment and the relative
neglect of better shopping opportunities in surrounding,
newer areas (Ministry of Housing and Local Government, 1969).
With the rapid rise in car ownership at this time it meant
that many town centres were faced with serious problems of
congestion which could not be alleviated simply by consumers
of their own accord going elsewhere where it was less
congested: to go anywhere else that was still convenient all
too often meant a sharp decline in shopping opportunity. The

90

government's approach was twofold: to improve town centre accessibility in terms of traffic circulation, new roads and multi-storey car parks and/or promote district, or second-tier, centres serving a minimum of 20 000 - 40 000 people in existing and new suburban areas. In either case it meant the promotion or modification of the existing retail hierarchy. At no time did the Ministry either seriously consider any major departures from this in terms of free-standing, privately sponsored, out-of-town centres, although there are plenty of portents of this type of development. The United States and Canada had seen these centres accompany suburban residential growth and increased car ownership for nearly twenty years; and the proposal and subsequent inquiry at Haydock Park in Lancashire (University of Manchester, Department of Town and Country Planning, 1964; Department of the Environment, 1965), as well as the heightening interest of other developers, indicated that the British government could soon be faced with similar types of pressure.

It was becoming increasingly apparent to the government that given the strategy of the 1947 Town and Country Planning Act and the structure of local government (in particular the separate planning powers between county boroughs and their surrounding counties and numerous county boroughs in close proximity), a very piecemeal and inefficient approach to development was often taking place. The Shopping Capacity Sub-Committee (N.E.D.O., 1971) and Mills (1974) note that from the point of view of retailing it was difficult to obtain some kind of regional strategy. Consumer behaviour did not confine itself to political boundaries! Yet there was a woefully inadequate system whereby local planning authorities co-ordinated their efforts to enhance the inter-urban retail hierarchy and prevent overprovision in certain retail sectors and underprovision in others.

The problem was addressed in three ways. First, after the early 1960s, a clearer commitment was made to regional development, and in the ensuing years a number of regional and sub-regional groups were initiated to undertake planning studies and make proposals to the government. The extent to which retailing was considered will be examined in 6.3 below. Unfortunately, without a corresponding electoral base in regional governments, the efforts of these groups remained advisory, often too academic and remote and conflicted with local authority intentions. After the election of a Conservative government in 1979 the regional advisory role was largely dropped.

Second, the Town and Country Planning Act, 1968 (amended in 1971) radically altered the existing planning process (Hall, 1974; Solesbury, 1975). Instead of the single, detailed plans outlining future land use proposals (with updating every five years supposedly), a two-tier process was proposed with structure plans, concentrating on broad policy statements for a large area and subject to central government approval, and local plans dovetailed into these, outlining detailed proposals for smaller areas on a more *ad hoc* basis and less subject to central government direction. This system of

planning led to a greater city-county co-operation and further
hastened local government reform.

Third, both Labour and Conservative governments in the 1960-
75 period were committed to local government reform, although
the process was slow, and while the outcome marked an
improvement, it in many ways fell short of what was needed.
Reform commenced with Greater London in 1964 but it was not
until 1974 that new local authorities began operating in the
rest of the country. Instead of large regional authorities[1],
which would have perhaps matched the regional strategies that
were suggested, a two-tier local government system was
established throughout of counties and metropolitan counties
with a small number of districts at the local level[2]. At
least the proliferation of small authorities was abolished;
but animosity still existed between the large cities (and
former county boroughs) and the counties in which they now
found themselves. The counties themselves all too often
followed historic boundaries, and metropolitan counties did
not encompass the outer suburbs and dormitory towns; thus
the authority of the upper tier of local government bore
little resemblance to modern day planning needs. In general,
local government reform formalised the new planning machinery
Structure plans were based on counties or areas of counties,
while local plans were undertaken at the district level.

However, as in the case of the old development plans the
central government has left it to the local planning
authorities in their structure plans to set up policy and
establish proposals, priorities and phasing, with respect to
the existing hierarchy of centres, town centre growth and new
centres, the quantity of floorspace and its distribution. To
the extent that the central government intervened or advised,
it would appear that it was not prepared to do anything that
would upset the status quo or unduly offend local government
wishes. In spite of pronouncements on developing district
centres to relieve central area congestion, it can be seen
that ever increasing amounts of money were still being spent
by central government on Comprehensive Development Area
schemes, which involve retailing, in town centres. Outside

---

[1] The Redcliffe-Maud Commission in 1969 proposed a pattern of
large unitary (one-tier) authorities for England, resembling
counties or city regions, with a two-tier system, modelled on
Greater London, for the Birmingham, Manchester and Liverpool
conurbations. However, the Conservative government, in their
local government reforms which became law in 1972, reaffirmed
the two-tier structure based on much smaller units.

[2] The Conservative government, in its speech from the throne
in June 1983, seems committed to abolishing the metropolitan
counties of Greater London, the West Midlands, Merseyside,
Greater Manchester, South Yorkshire, West Yorkshire and Tyne
and Wear; in effect, turning the clock back to 1974 and the
reign of the county boroughs, and in the London case to even
the pre-London County Council era.

the new town schemes there has been little government encouragement of district centre development, and where it has taken place it has often made minimal impact on central area congestion. The Shopping Capacity Sub-Committee early on suggested that most district centre development would have greater impact on existing suburban retail facilities (N.E.D.O., 1971). As for innovative features such as out-of-town shopping centres and stores the central government was not opposed in principle; but on the other hand it did not direct that local authorities should take account of this type of development in its structure plans and propose sites on the fringes of urban areas in its local plans. The result was therefore to pass the problem over to the local arena.

The best the central government would do, in the absence of a firm commitment for or against out-of-town centres, was to take up the Shopping Capacity Sub-Committee on its suggestion of giving guidelines to local authorities stating criteria for the acceptability of such centres. The Development Control Policy Note that followed (Department of the Environment, 1972c) set out government policy not merely on out-of-town centres but on a whole range of issues (e.g. green belt development and transportation) which could also be affected should an out-of-town centre be built. It was also stressed that the purpose of the note was to give general guidance to all those concerned in the operation of planning control (i.e. what to do if and when the eventuality arose) rather than planning for future shopping needs. Furthermore, and this was shown in 5.2, the central government fully intended to treat each planning application or appeal on its merits, and in the application of a general policy to a particular case it made allowance for judgment for or against on the part of those having the power of approval at whatever level.

The policy note clearly indicates the caution that the central government has always adopted, but underlying it one can see a certain ambivalent attitude. In the introduction it is suggested that out-of-town shopping centres contribute to lower retail prices, greater convenience to car-borne consumers and relieving traffic congestion; on the other hand, they can cause a loss of rural amenity, unduly influence existing centres and produce new traffic problems on inter-urban and rural roads. Thus the policy note is designed to elucidate for local planning authorities, retailers and developers the advantages and disadvantages that need to be weighed against each other in considering each proposal: it is in no way a directive to local planning authorities to plan in such a way as to maximise the former and minimise the latter.

The first note of caution surrounds the availability of the car for shopping. It was expected that at least 25 per cent of families will lack cars by 1980 (an underestimate), and those dependent on public transport might not be able to benefit from car oriented, out-of-town shopping. Therefore, should existing centres decline as a result, then a certain section of the community would be disadvantaged. It is suggested that well planned district centres would better be able to sustain good public transport.

Second, the government states that all parties will need to assess the consequences in terms of existing shopping should out-of-town shopping centres be built; although the remarks are prefaced by the fact that it is not government policy to use land use planning to prevent competition between retailers or methods of retailing nor to preserve existing retail centre It is concerned that new shopping forms will create an over-provision of shops on a large scale and result in a decline of shops in existing centres which will have serious economic social, financial and other planning consequences.

A third note of caution relates to other consequences that are likely, including the harmful effects on amenity and public services, which were considered in detail in Chapter 4, the departures from existing development plan provisions and the likely spin-off effects in terms of an out-of-town centre attracting other development into the vicinity.

The guidelines say virtually nothing about the advantages of out-of-town centres, except by way of introduction; and in setting out what the various parties should look for when considering proposals, they play upon the many negative aspects. It could be argued that certain characteristics call for a more positive vein and better direction in planning for future shopping needs:

i) local authorities and retailers in existing centres hardly need the cautionary note since the majority are already sufficiently dubious or opposed to out-of-town centres that most of the arguments that would enable a proposal to be defeated are already well known;

ii) so many proposals are forthcoming and some have been approved, or are likely to be approved, that out-of-town centres will have a significant impact anyway on future shopping patterns, and where local authorities stand in the way of this type of development, it may encourage less than satisfactory alternatives (e.g. legal or illegal warehouse conversions);

iii) a number of wider social and economic forces are resultin in a change in consumer attitudes towards shopping behaviour, changes which can perhaps more adequately and more efficiently be catered for in out-of-town centres rather than existing centres.

The guidelines leave too much unsaid which would in the circumstances help to promote out-of-town centres not only by highlighting their advantages but also by dampening the effects on the existing retail system and pointing out the possible collision course should the existing system not be sufficiently modified to suit future needs. Local planning authorities and retailers were expected to operate in a climate where little was known at the time about the impact of out-of-town centres, and both groups tended to (conveniently) overestimate the effects that such centres would have. Moreover, the government was very slow to initiate any impact studies, leaving it to others to do so; and as was shown in Chapter 3 the results were piecemeal and have not diffused

well to those local authorities and retailers who are faced
with out-of-town centre proposals.

Too much play is made in the guidelines concerning the 25
per cent of households who will not have cars rather than
the majority who will have them. Besides, given sufficient
incentives, it is possible to provide most out-of-town centres
with reasonable public transport; and it is important not to
forget that many centres, placed conveniently with respect
to residential development, perform the role of a district
or neighbourhood centre and attract a large proportion of
consumers who walk to shop.

While stress is laid upon not using land use planning to
prevent competition between retailer and retail methods, the
government's cautionary stance, coupled with the inherent
opposition at the local level where initial decisions are
allowed to be made, give at least *de facto* recognition to
the claim that government is promoting the existing retail
system. Furthermore, the tremendous investment of public
money in town centre redevelopment schemes, for example, and
the consequences in other areas should these falter, is further
evidence of government support for the status quo.   The
strong and persistent desire of government to discourage the
overprovision of shopping facilities may be good for certain
economic and planning reasons, but it naturally gives undue
advantage to those in the field first (i.e. the existing
retail facilities), interferes with normal market forces and
may give rise to the persistence of a more inefficient and
more costly retail system. One could appreciate the overprovision argument more if it was better applied, but
government policy and timing of development has often
generously allowed for overprovision within the existing
retail system.

The guidelines show the somewhat confused government policy
with respect to traffic implications, more especially in
town centres. That out-of-town centre proposals should be
considered in the light of the adequate measures being taken
to accommodate car traffic in town centres says nothing about
the cost effectiveness and environmental impact of trying to
adapt town centres to take more traffic, and whether it would
not be better to promote new shopping patterns or restrict
car access in town centres. The further problem arises that
retail development and improved accessibility and car parking
are the responsibility of different groups, and the lack of
co-ordination in timing and differential restrictions in
money supply, such that the latter falls behind the former,
can place further stresses on town centre redevelopment.

Finally, the guidelines can be variously interpreted by the
different parties concerned and are perhaps a licence to
back up a previously held notion at the local level. This
is understandable when the guidelines focus on development
specifically for (or against) out-of-town centres.

Government policy, where so much of the responsibility is abdicated to the local level through development control, poses further problems. It virtually precludes any regional strategy, even allowing for larger and fewer local authorities First of all, the district councils are the local planning authorities, and it is often possible to make decisions at this level without intervention by other government levels where the likelihood of a regional strategy could be better achieved. Second, there is no guarantee that the eventual locations of out-of-town centres are the best possible; it is more likely to be paths of least resistance. Since such centres are the responsibility of the private sector, it might be thought possible to project a regional strategy by examining where the developer seeks to locate. However, part of any developer's planning would be the realisation ahead of time whether or not an application stood any chance of success. Those planning applications which come forward for consideration are only a proportion of those the developers would like to see; these applications are the ones which are more likely not to be rejected out of hand, i.e. do not conflict with too many government guidelines and are not in areas where local government is openly hostile and or similar applications have been previously refused. The one exception to the 'location where the local authority approves' notion is the approval by the Secretary of State following an appeal on a local authority refusal (see 5.2). However these decisions contribute only a small minority. What one can see, on the other hand, is a very sporadic diffusion of the out-of-town shopping centre. The majority of the population, and especially those in the highest car-ownership areas, have no easy access to any one, whilst some areas are faced with competing facilities.

It is possible through the planning appeal mechanism for the central government to become more involved in the policy are and give backing to its guidelines. But this is less than satisfactory. It depends first of all on the local authorit refusing an application, and secondly a developer then appealing. To fill the void the government has the right to call in applications under certain conditions (see 5.2). But the appeal procedure is too much like the initial approval procedure, i.e. each application is judged on its own merits for there to be much in the way of overall, consistent approac towards out-of-town centres. Besides the government guidelines to developers, retailers and local authorities also apply to planning inspectors and its own departmental officials; and thus government policy, which examines out-of-town centres i the light of their effect on existing centres and various aspects of urban and rural amenity, still prevails.

The dearth of a commitment to out-of-town centres by the government and the lack of better regional strategies promote uncertainty amongst existing retailers and local authorities whether or not they in fact favour such centres. Those who oppose might be thought to welcome government policy and the allowance of local autonomy to make decisions; but should planning appeals or government call-ins result, there can be considerable delay before a decision is made (Lee and Kent,

1976; 1978) which can affect planning in other areas.
Moreover, since planning appeal decisions afford the
opportunity for external independent assessments, there is
no knowing whether planning inspectors and the Secretary of
State will see the situation in the same way as the local
authority. There was a very real fear, following the local
authority's rejection of all out-of-town centres to the west
of Colchester (Department of the Environment, 1977b), that
the planning inspector or the Secretary of State, in
considering each case on its own merits, could recommend the
approval of two, even all three, centres where an appeal was
held.

There has been no appreciable change in central government
policy and attitudes towards out-of-town centres during the
1970s. Knowledge of their impact, gained from the studies
that have been undertaken of individual centres, resulted in
the government allowing more local autonomy by raising the
notification level to 100 000 sq.ft. (Department of the
Environment, 1976b). Local authorities were at this time
given a summary of the Secretary of State's reasons for
refusing or approving those planning applications coming to
him after 1972. However, it is not known how this is
supposed to help local authorities, since the reasons for
acceptance or rejection are numerous, difficult to rank order
and impossible to compare from one case to another (simply
because comparisons are never intended in the first place).

In 1976 the government contacted local authorities concerning
revisions to its 1972 Policy Note. The resulting statement
(Department of the Environment, 1977a) updates a number of
issues (e.g. from 1 in 4 without a car in 1980 to 1 in 3 in
1985) and gives more detail (e.g. the traditional pattern of
shopping centres), but the same overall doubts are raised
concerning out-of-town centres. It recognises that certain
functions and scales of retail operation may prefer new types
of retail location; but it is not possible to consider these
in isolation, and it also suggests, or intimates, that the
district centre could provide many of the same advantages,
as well as better opportunities in some areas (e.g. public
transport provision). Any retail development not in a
traditional centre must still be carefully reviewed in terms
of its need (and doubt is cast here concerning the use of
mathematical models) and its influence on overall planning
proposals, the existing retail hierarchy, traffic and highway
considerations, adjacent land uses and urban and rural amenity.

The policy is still based on whether the out-of-town centre
can be fitted into the existing hierarchy with minimal
disturbance, if and when a proposal is put forth, rather than
stating that such centres should be planned for in terms of
future shopping needs and giving guidance as to what, where/
where not and when and the factors which should determine
these. However, where the government is more involved in
the retail decision-making process, for example in new towns,
there has been a better accommodation first of all of
innovative ideas in terms of location and shopping centre
and store design and second co-operation with the private

sector (many of whom are in out-of-town centre developments) who in effect become the tenants of a publicly owned scheme. The Carrefour hypermarket which had created so much controversy at Caerphilly became the accepted centre-piece in the initial development at the Telford New Town Centre. In appearance, with acres of surface car parking and the absence of surrounding commercial or residential development at the time, the centre resembled a private out-of-town shopping centre. It would seem that the real weakness of the government's policy lies in leaving too much of the decision making at the local level with the abiding emphasis on development control.

6.3   SUB-REGIONAL PLANNING

Given the central government's policy, attitudes and degree of involvement in retail planning, it follows that policy at a more local level is of particular importance when it becomes to the development, or lack of development, of out-of-town centres. Some of the more important ideas in terms of how and what to plan for in retailing came from the many sub-regional plans that were commenced in the 1960s (Jackson, 1972).[1] These plans resulted from various contiguous local authorities, in the absence of better local government units seeing a need for co-operation in planning for future development on a more integrated basis. (The government afterwards made changes in the Town and Country Planning Act and local government structure to further aid these improvements.) Most of the plans employed, or developed, various techniques in mathematical modelling to forecast future demands (for population, employment, housing, shopping etc.), in total and by sub-area, using a complex series of socio-economic variables which themselves needed to be predicted.

From the point of view of retailing Jackson (1972) noted that two approaches were adopted in planning for existing and new shopping centres. First, variations of the retail gravity model were used to predict the location and hierarchy of centres in a region based on results from a future distribution of population. Second, an *a priori* approach was used where a desired retail hierarchy was seen as a planning objective and many of the other changes were proposed with this in mind. Both approaches suffer some very basic weaknesses in that the socio-economic variables used in the models, or assumed in the hierarchy design, were too limited. Little account was often taken of changes, or likely changes, in corporate and consumer behaviour arising from other socio-economic change; for example, rationalisation and the demand for fewer but larger retail units, increased mobility through car ownership

---

[1] The specific plans referred to relate to the following areas: Teeside, Leicester and Leicestershire, Nottinghamshire and Derbyshire, North Gloucestershire, Coventry-Solihull-Warwickshire, South Hampshire and Humberside.

declining frequency in convenience-good purchasing and the increased demand for one-stop shopping.

A common theme in all the sub-regional plans, and one that is now quite familiar, was to do little that would in anyway jeopardise the existing retail structure: proposed changes would affect relative positions but would for the most part not lead to drastic decline in any retail centre. The traditional retail hierarchy was upheld, and new major shopping centres were closely tied to new residential development to promote it still further. In some instances (Leicester and Leicestershire, Nottinghamshire and Derbyshire and South Hampshire) it was proposed that retail facilities would not be overly concentrated in town centres, but that decentralisation into regional centres would provide the more dispersed city region with improved accessibility. Elsewhere, it was expected that town centres such as Gloucester, Middlesborough and Coventry would grow substantially.

Free-standing, private out-of-town centres were given little credence in many of the studies. In Nottinghamshire and Derbyshire, for example, it was considered that there was already a well established retail pattern and new residential developments had easy access to this (Nottingham-Derbyshire Sub-Regional Planning Unit, 1969). In South Hampshire future retail development was to be concentrated in various sub-regional centres with the expansion of district centres in five of the six growth areas (South Hampshire Plan Advisory Committee, 1972a). It recognised that there may be the need for a strictly limited number of free-standing car-based stores (of approximately 60 000-80 000 sq.ft. gross) to complement existing centres, but thought given the physical opportunities and build-up of trading potential that it was unlikely that such stores would be needed until the late 1970s or early 1980s (South Hampshire Plan Advisory Committee, 1972b). As was noted in 2.6 something was amiss in the Committee's thinking since the local planning authority had already been faced with a proposal for an out-of-town hypermarket at Chandlers Ford. It was initially rejected because it did not fit the structure plan as proposed; never was it considered that the hypermarket could substitute for a district centre (or be an additional centre) in an area that was crying out for more retail facilities anyway. In North Gloucestershire the sub-regional plan study actually postulated a large free-standing retail development between Gloucester and Cheltenham at Staverton but pulled back because the viability of existing centres, especially Cheltenham, would be affected (Gloucestershire C.C., Gloucester C.C. and Cheltenham B.C., 1970). Jackson (1972) detected a general unwillingness to consider innovative forms of retailing and warned that the traditional habits of retailing are not sacrosanct.

6.4 COUNTY AND DISTRICT PLANNING

The sub-regional plans were far from universal in their coverage and can be viewed as a stop-gap measure until such time as local government and planning reforms took place.

But as noted in 6.2 the new system of local government that was in operation by 1974 fell short of what was perhaps needed. In keeping so strictly to historic county boundaries and in confining the new metropolitan counties to older built-up areas, it made the adoption of regional or sub-regional planning strategies very difficult over much of the country. In retailing, for example, the major catchment area for some town centres can overrun two or more county authorities and thus the future viability of that centre can be affected, perhaps significantly, without there being very effective ways of preventing it. Moreover, there is still a likelihood of overprovision of shopping facilities by counting the same consumers more than once, a problem that can be exacerbated as personal mobility increases. It is therefore important that emphasis be placed on regional and sub-regional studies so that county-wide structure plans can be integrated and potential conflicts eliminated.

At present, however, the main initiatives in land use and policy planning lie at the county and district levels. The counties are largely responsible for structure planning and establishing overall policy and development strategies, although the emphasis is often on land use rather than policy; while the districts are responsible for the more detailed land use planning to be found in local plans and the administration of development control. In the case of the latter planning applications need to be referred to county planners for comment should they conflict with strategic planning policy. It is at these two levels, in terms of setting out policy, designating land use and administering development control, that the main initiatives have come (albeit tentatively) in establishing out-of-town shopping centres. Since the central government has handed over so much of the responsibility of retail planning to the local level, it is not surprising that the initiatives have been few: Chapter 5 showed that local politicians, small businessmen and professional staff, largely remain adamantly opposed to this type of innovative retailing. Two of these groups have a fundamental role to play in establishing policy and approving plans and planning permissions.

Structure planning, thus far, has shown concern for shopping policy formulation, but there is little awareness of trends in corporate and consumer behaviour and a tendency, therefore, to reinforce the present retail hierarchy and design and locate new shopping centres to fit in with this and new residential development. This reinforcement has come principally in the promotion of town centre retailing, the reasons for which were discussed in 5.3. It is interesting to note that many structure plans, despite the many retail impact studies that are available, still blindly state the belief that to allow free-standing out-of-town centres would seriously erode the viability of these town centres. In many instances structure plans do take note of the serious problems of overreliance on town centres, but for the most part the remedy is the district centre associated with suburban overspill housing developments. However, it can be seen that what is meant by a district centre can vary considerably from one local authority to the

next. Some district centres are so small or physically
inadequate (e.g. inner city, ribbon, small shops or fringe-
area former warehouses) that they cannot hope to offer
sufficient a range of comparison goods to take much of the
pressure off a nearby town centre. Moreover, even for
convenience goods there may still be considerable movement
to a town centre, since the district centre supermarket is
smaller and prices are most likely higher. At the other
end of the scale it has been noted that the large district
centre can perform the role of a free-standing out-of-town
centre with the added advantage that the former can be planned
for in a more comprehensive fashion and quite possibly owned
and operated by the local authority.

There is a marked reluctance for structure plans to take
account of out-of-town centres, even where transportation
changes have influenced mobility, the actions or intentions
of developers are known, and even more ironically after a
proposal has received approval from the Secretary of State
for the Environment. In such instances it has been common
to use the formulation of a structure plan as an excuse for
a local planning authority not to approve an out-of-town
centre, the reasoning being that it would be premature to
give approval since to do so may seriously jeopardise the
eventual policies and proposals laid out in the structure
plan. Planning inspectors and the Secretary of State have
generally not been too impressed by the prematurity argument
(see, for example, Department of the Environment, 1972b).
First of all structure planning has taken up to ten years or
more to reach fruition, and it would be unreasonable (or
rather totally impossible) to hold all development in abeyance
until a structure plan is approved. Second, it is recognised
that local authorities are invariably being selective in their
application of the prematurity argument: it is so often used
only for proposals with which they do not agree. Third, no
form of planning can be so inflexible that new types of
retailing (or change in any other form of land use for that
matter) cannot result in readjustments to previously held or
approved policies and plans. It can be argued that the
majority of out-of-town centre proposals are of a type that
would not result in serious readjustments anyway. Finally,
the reverse argument, that it is an opportune time to consider
a proposal, may be more true. To give permission now rather
than later gives a local authority more time to make adjustments
to its structure plan submissions. However, the prematurity
argument in any planning application can only stand a chance
of being challenged should the refusal be appealed.

A second aspect to this reluctance to consider out-of-town
centres relates to the myriad of objections that have been
raised from various quarters. They can range from the
protectionist views seen in 5.3 to the more objective
considerations of land use and retail conflicts contained in
the government's policy notes (Department of the Environment,
1972c, 1976b). In the absence of any firm directives from
the government to take such retail innovations into account,
it becomes apparent, even for local authorities which are
favourably disposed towards out-of-town centres, that very

101

soon at least one of the many objections will intervene to
help disqualify either any consideration of out-of-town
centres or specific locations.

Some light at the end of the tunnel can be seen in those
structure plans which while not condoning a complete free-
for-all in the retail sector, on the other hand do not
condemn out-of-town centres out of hand. There may be a
strong intention to protect town centres but not to overly
concentrate retail facilities there to the detriment of the
centre's handling capacity and retail facilities or proposals
elsewhere. Meanwhile it is recognised that the out-of-town
centre can perform much of the role of a district centre and
can be just as well located with respect to population areas.

It can be seen that some county authorities are not necessarily
opposed to the idea of out-of-town centres, but on the other
hand they either feel ill-equipped or otherwise hesitant about
becoming involved in their structure planning. It is argued
that it is hard to plan for something where virtually all the
initiatives lie in the private sector; even identifying
suitable areas for development would reinforce the public
priorities of promoting overall social benefit, whereas the
developer is more likely to choose areas which maximise access
to market and thus profit. Moreover, to identify such areas
may be seen as unfair, since it may introduce more retail
competition into one area than another. As the government
have in effect allowed the out-of-town centre phenomenon to
be a development control matter, it may appear more realistic
for county authorities not to be unduly concerned in their
structure planning but to let local authorities take account
of the problem either in their own local plans or when
considering planning applications. Some structure plans,
therefore, are more concerned with future retail needs in
terms of broad floorspace requirements within various districts
rather than specify the exact type of retail facility and
where it should go. Abdicating the responsibility for more
detailed policy making to the district level, however, is
almost tantamount, given the record so far, of inviting the
rejection of out-of-town centres.

Two-tier local government and the nature of the division of
planning responsibilities can lead to conflicts in the policy-
making and decision-making process, particularly where a
planning application has to be referred to the county
authority. A further weakness in the way policies have been
formulated with respect to out-of-town centres is that in
judging each case on its own merits, it is possible for
county and district authorities to differ in their decisions.
While it can be argued that this is now a healthier process
than the earlier situation where, for example, county and
county borough often worked in isolation, it could be
improved upon if the policy roles were more clearly delineated
or more of the responsibilities for planning and development
control were passed to the county authority. A divergence of
opinion between county and district authorities gives a
developer a chance to exploit a situation to his own advantage;
at a planning inquiry, for example, the developer can use the

appropriate plan information and committee and council decisions at the county level, which express support or no objection, to back up his case against a local authority planning refusal.

The planning inquiry into the Sainsbury superstore proposal on the west side of Colchester is indicative of the type of conflict that can arise (Department of the Environment, 1977b). Part of Sainsbury's evidence before the inquiry included details of Essex County Council's policies and opinions on the matter, which could easily be interpreted as being in a state of flux, compared to earlier statements, and not wholly against out-of-town centres. In the first review of the County Development Plan (submitted in 1965 and approved in 1976) it was county policy to concentrate major new shopping developments in town centres. Out-of-town centres were considered the outcome of conditions, more prevalent in North America than in Essex, where there had been a rapid spread of low density residential development, high car useage, poor or non-existent public transport, more one-stop shopping and a far weaker commitment to the protection of rural amenity. Besides adapting the town centres to meet new demands, district shopping centres (four in the case of Colchester) would also be promoted. This policy was amended in 1972 when it was noted that shopping habits have changed and off-centre stores with adjacent car parks probably have a place in future shopping provision. However, there was no good reason to permit them outside the built-up area, and they should be seen as replacements to old shopping parades or adaptations of district centres. In the preparation later of the Essex Structure Plan the question of out-of-town centres is considered in broad terms, and it is noted that whether or not Colchester's town centre should be supplemented by off-centre stores must be considered. When Sainsbury's actual proposal was referred to the Development Control Sub-Committee of the Essex County Council it was recommended that since there were no county policy objections to the superstore and its location, no case be made at the planning inquiry. The District Council, on the other hand, in defending their refusal to grant planning permission, only raised the matter of county policy for the period up to 1972; the veiled support, or at least the need for consideration, contained in county policy after that was largely ignored.

A further area of conflict between the two levels of government in Essex, which the developer exploited, concerned a problem noted earlier, namely what actually constitutes a district centre. In the first review of the County Development Plan four district centres of certain sizes were proposed in Colchester, but no actual site was pinpointed for the one on the west side of the town. The developer argued that since the superstore was approximately the size envisaged in the Development Plan and in the same general location, and furthermore that suitable alternatives were lacking on this west side, permission should be given. The County Council in effect concurred that the superstore substituted for a district centre when it declined to become involved in the planning inquiry. Colchester's Planning Officer reiterated

the same sentiments when reporting to the District Council's
Planning Committee, adding that the store was well related
to residential areas for pedestrian traffic and not causing
further extensions to the built-up area since the site had
already been approved for housing development. However, the
District Council later argued that the superstore was not
needed since existing shopping facilities dispersed throughout
the area (a Co-op discount store in a former warehouse, two
smaller supermarkets and two small shopping parades)
constituted the equivalent of a district centre. (For various
reasons seen in 5.3 the District Council was obviously burying
its head in the sand or desperate for any argument to defeat
the Sainsbury proposal if it was prepared to promote the
existing facilities as a district centre; and the planning
inspector concluded that existing facilities could never meet
modern shopping needs.)

The timeing of structure-local planning and the consideration of
retail innovations present two divergent pictures. Mills (1974)
suggested that structure planning was proceeding too slowly
at a time when new retail development applications were
coming at a rapid pace and there was no firm government policy
in existence to help local authorities. Apart from encouraging
the use of the prematurity argument as a delaying tactic, it
is questionable whether such tardiness significantly affects
the ongoing planning process, especially in the case of out-
of-town centres which largely remain an *ad hoc* development
control procedure. On the other hand, whilst structure
planning has been progressing at such a slow pace, there has
been some change of policy or attitude on retail developments
on the part of local government. In the 1960 most development
plans, if they mentioned out-of-town centres at all, did so
unfavourably since there was limited knowledge and even more
limited experience. But more recently there has been a
greater recognition of the issues involved. More is known
about the impact of such centres, at least, by professional
staff, and many have been built since the 1970s and have
proved that they do not have a disastrous effect on the
existing retail structure. However, it can be argued that
in the final analysis, i.e. the approved structure plan,
opposition to such centres remain as great as ever.

Any progress in policy making and attitudes perhaps needs to
be accompanied by appropriate land use modifications at the
local level. There is a marked reluctance as yet to plan for
out-of-town centres by identifying possible sites or types of
site, on the urban fringe. This results in the developer
taking one of three possible courses of action: i) invading,
or attempting to invade, an area used or designated for
warehouse or light industrial development (often to the
dissatisfaction of both the developer and the local authority);
ii) joining forces with the local authority to plan for and
build a traditional district, or neighbourhood, centre as
part of a residential expansion; and iii) seeking planning
permission to build on land not currently used or designated
for urban purposes. The last of these is no substitute for
the local authority designating the land or possible areas
beforehand; the developer's location could represent some

line of least resistance rather than the most desired
location. The marked reluctance may simply reflect inertia,
a lack of imagination or foresight, or perhaps the feeling
that to designate sites would increase the likelihood of
having the problem in one's midst.

6.5 CONCLUSION

In this chapter an attempt has been made to show that
government involvement in the retail sector in general and
the out-of-town centre problem in particular has been limited
and confusing. There has been considerable hesitancy about
obtaining a good data base on which to formulate policy and
make judgments in the first place; and while this was
achieved elsewhere, the tendency has been for the central
government to err on the side of caution or favour the status
quo. Rather than give directives and information to local
authorities about planning for out-of-town centres, the
central government has merely issued somewhat ambiguous
guidelines to help local authorities deal with applications
for planning permission, stressing that at whatever stage in
the planning process an application must be treated primarily
on its own merits. In the absence of more and better central
government involvement the major initiatives on shopping and
shopping centre policy must be undertaken at a more local
level. However, this frequently precludes the adoption of
better regional strategies and the eradication of problems
such as under or overprovision of retail facilities. To
some extent changes to the Town and Country Planning Act and
the structure of local government have helped in this regard;
but these two factors alone cannot overcome the long standing
opposition to out-of-town centres that seems so prevalent at
this level. The tendency is to deal with the problem if and
when it arises and meanwhile to promote the traditional
retail hierarchy. More recently there are indications that
structure planning is giving greater consideration to out-of-
town centres, but there is some way to go before the sentiment
is anywhere near universal or it has been translated into
appropriate land use planning at the local level.

7. Prospects for the 1980s and beyond

In this chapter an attempt is made to discuss the changes
currently taking place, or which could take place, with
respect to out-of-town centre shopping, given various social,
economic and political forces (which themselves are undergoing
change). Discussion will focus first of all on these forces
which have been so instrumental in retail change in the past
that one cannot see any likelihood that they will not play a
similar role in the future. Second, how these forces are
allowed to influence retailing and consumer behaviour will
depend in part on government policies relating to land use
planning. Third, retail organisation, the way in which
business is carried on and the non-spatial element in this
discussion, will be examined in the light of both these wider
societal forces and government policies. This in turn will
lead to various pressures for change in the retail hierarchy
itself; and given the spatial nature of this hierarchy, various
aspects of retail location that are likely to arise will be
discussed.

Whilst one can forsee the types of change likely to take
place in retailing in Britain, this is not to say that these
will occur everywhere with ease. If the past is any
indication, forward thinking on the part of government to
accommodate innovation will be variously lacking. In the
retail case the cumbersome and inconsistent machinery of
planning, its strength at the local scale where vested
interests in the old ways are so strong and the weaknesses
of central government in promoting innovation will continue
to encourage a retail environment that is fraught with
problems. The more important of these will be highlighted
in the sections below. It can be seen that Britain is
presently undergoing a series of political changes where
private enterprise, market forces, monetarism and the freedom
of the individual to do (almost) what he wants are being
encouraged in place of the heavily government dependent
society that has developed since the Second World War. The
question arises, how will this extend to the retail sector
of the economy, and to what extent will there be the almost
free-for-all which is so characteristic of North American
society, for example, where innovations are embraced far more
easily. Sufficient chinks in the armour can perhaps be seen
already to indicate that these political changes will either
be far from universal in the British economy, or, given the

inherent conservatism of British society, will take a
considerable time to achieve: retailing, one strongly
suspects, will be one of these.

7.1 THE WIDER FORCES OF CHANGE

Retail innovations, and more specifically developments in
out-of-town shopping, are not islands unto themselves. They
have been influenced by wider social, economic and political
forces, and as these forces change, many aspects of British
society, retailing and consumer behaviour included, are
likely to change also. These wider forces of change can be
identified as follows:

Changes in the economy The cycle of boom and bust, which
has been so characteristic of Western economies since the
Second World War, affects the supply of money for capital
investment, building and development and the purchase of
goods and services. Much of the planning and development of
major shopping schemes, principally in town centres, took
place in the boom years of the 1960s and early 1970s. However,
the falling off of such schemes later in the 1970s is not
simply associated with the recession that set in after the
world oil crisis in 1973. There could be a state of
saturation and therefore a fall off in demand for new
development, an interest in development in new locations and
a change of attitude by both the public and private sector
in the relative merits of town centre development (Guy, 1980).

It can be seen that the recession of the 1970s and 1980s has
resulted in an overall decline, or a slowing down of the
increase, in many economic and social indicators; but in no
way has this been universal. While there has been a slowing
down of large schemes in town centres, the pressures for
development of various types of suburban shopping have not
abated. Britain is simply too far behind other developed
nations, and therefore far from a state of saturation, for
there to be any let-up in this pressure. In the case of
hypermarket and superstore developments, whether in out-of-
town or district centre locations, there are still large
areas of the country and major centres of population such as
Greater London lacking this particular retail innovation; and
even allowing for harsh and uncertain economic times, there
are still numerous proposals from the major multiple firmsto
fill the gaps (Department of the Environment, 1981b; Jones,
P., 1981; Jones, P.M., 1982; Unit for Retail Planning
Information, 1982).

The general economic situation is not a good indicator of
what might transpire in terms of out-of-town shopping. Indeed,
Britain could come out of its recession and find some types
of development then falling off because a saturation point
had been reached. Also, the economic malaise of Britain in
the 1980s should not be allowed to mask the fact that living
standards have been rising in real terms, at least amongst
those who are still in employment. This will no doubt
heighten the geography of inequality in Britain; and it is
fair to say that it will be middle class populations in outer

surburban and outer- metropolitan areas (i.e. those more
likely to avail themselves of out-of-town shopping facilities) who will benefit most from improved living standards.
Entrepreneurs in the various out-of-town shopping developments, therefore, have little reason to fear market forces.

Changes in energy resources Changes in the economy have been
closely associated since the early 1970s with changes in the
supply and demand of energy resources. Because retailers
and consumers use energy in the development and running of
stores and shopping centres and getting themselves and their
goods to and from the stores, any change in the supply side
of energy will affect retail and consumer behaviour. The
oil crises of the 1970s, with the sharply increased prices
faced by Western countries and the likelihood of grave
shortages and rationing, were at first considered likely to
place car travel in severe jeopardy; and, therefore, car-
related activities, such as out-of-town shopping, would also
be affected. However, faltering economies, increasing energy
conservation and falling demand have broken the back of the
oil supply cartels; prices have fallen on world markets,
shortages and rationing have been almost non-existent and
car travel has been little affected. At first opponents of
out-of-town shopping developments jumped on the energy
conservation bandwagon; but as the need to preserve energy
became less apparent and less critical and consumers adjusted
to ever increasing prices at the pumps, this argument fell
by the wayside.

In the long term it is realised that the energy situation
will never return to its pre 1973 position. On the other
hand, the likelihood of energy resources running out, foreign
countries holding Britain to ransom and doom ensuing for the
car owner are just as unlikely. The strength, even necessity
of car travel are such that alternate energy resources would
become economically viable and politically opportune to
sustain car travel before there was any stampede back to bus
and train travel. The out-of-town shopping developer need
have little fear that his market will suddenly evaporate. On
the contrary, there is a large population out there just
waiting to join that market.

Changes in technology Science and business are constantly
seeking ways to improve existing technologies by adapting or
investing in new methods or new hardware and software. These
can be in the interest of academic achievement, consumer
satisfaction or personal/corporate profit and market share.
In the retail sector changing technology refers to a seemingl
endless list of innovative products and services, buildings
and other infrastructure changes, new supply, storage, display
and selling methods and the corporate reorganisation necessar
to promote these successfully. Experience has shown us that
it is invariably easier and cheaper (and not merely to the
developer!) to introduce innovative technologies into purpose
built shops and shopping centres on previously vacant sites,
rather than adapt existing premises or traditional retail
centres to perform the same task. The fact that so much
adaptation has taken place in existing British shopping

centres is more a testament to making the best of a bad job in the face of planning restrictions than it is to seeking the best possible solution for all concerned.

The ultimate in technological change would result in the redundancy of all types of retail location! This could occur when all information of goods and services would be sent to the home via various forms of telecommunication and the resulting purchase would be delivered either the same way or in person from a warehouse: the consumer would never need to leave the home. While this will no doubt take place for those who consider shopping a chore (just as it did when mail order, the telephone and the delivery boy/van were introduced), those who consider shopping a pleasure, a way to meet people, a way to occupy time or experiencing the real thing, will still constitute sufficient numbers to promote new centres and maintain most of the existing centres.

Changing consumer lifestyles It might be thought crystal ball gazing to suggest what consumers will demand in terms of goods and services many years hence. This may be so on the finer points of detail, but sufficient trends have been set in motion that cannot fail to diffuse to others. Even allowing for cultural variations, why should innovations started in North America or Western Europe and acceptable to consumers there not spread to Britain; within Britain, why should innovations adopted first by the middle class not spread down the social ladder; finally, something that is taken up by young married couples, for example, is bound to spread as that population ages, assuming, of course, that younger age groups take it up too.

A number of consumer lifestyle characteristics favour the development of out-of-town shopping centres. Perhaps the most important relates to the many factors surrounding consumer mobility. It has been shown above that fewer than 60 per cent of British households own at least one car and fewer than 10 per cent own two or more cars. Since these figures are higher in the wealthier and younger age groups, and correspondingly lower in the other groups, there is little doubt that overall figures will improve somewhat as the population ages and living standards and social mobility improve. Often where a car is available, it cannot be driven because the housewife lacks a driving licence. Again. this is a feature closely associated with age and income; as these change, access to the car and car-oriented shopping will improve. Given the high incidence and convenience of car use at out-of-town centres and the pressures that increasing car use will make on town centres, it is likely that the former location will gain at the relative or absolute expense of the latter.

Improved mobility and increasing car use go beyond merely car ownership. A car has become increasingly necessary (or perceived as necessary) in order for the consumer to carry out a certain lifestyle that incorporates shopping; and the bus, even where conveniently available (and this is increasingly not the case) just will not do. One-stop

shopping for everyday food and non-food items, the bulk and
weight of the purchases, the increasing family outing nature
of shopping, overall comfort and pressure on time promote
the use of the car and the convenience of the out-of-town
centre in receiving it. The out-of-town shopping centre
could decline if these reasons for using it change. This
does not seem likely even in the long term; but if it did
happen, the out-of-town centre could adapt, as town centres
have done, to new consumer demands.

The use of the car has been aided by a massive programme of
new and improved roads and associated works. The network of
new motorways and new and improved trunk routes, for example
have the potential of encouraging out-of-town shopping, and
thus influencing the retail hierarchy, as consumers equate
travel to shop with journey time rather than distance. The
importance of the Brent Cross Shopping Centre amongst
consumers to the north in Hertfordshire and Bedfordshire for
example, is related to the ease of travel via the M1 Motorway
(Shepherd and Newby, 1978). However, as will be seen below
this potential is far from being fully realised.

A further factor that suggests anything but a diminution in
out-of-town centre interest is consumer residential choice.
In spite of falling birth rates eventually reducing housing
demand and government interest in inner city renewal,
decentralisation to the suburbs and beyond is still popular
amongst those who can afford it and aspired to by those who
cannot. Moreover, there is no hope of the existing city,
and particularly the inner city, absorbing future population
and at the same time improving the living standards of the
present population. Thus, an increasing proportion of the
population will find town centre shopping less convenient
compared to out-of-town centres or even other town centres.

7.2 GOVERNMENT POLICIES AND LAND USE PLANNING

How the many changes taking place in these wider societal
forces will influence retail and consumer behaviour will
depend in part on government policies in the field of land
use planning. From the point of view of out-of-town shopping
centres, it has been shown in Chapter 6 that policies at
various government levels have been indifferent or
restrictive. If out-of-town centres have been built, they
have resulted from breaking through the development control
barrier at the local level, rather than being planned for in
terms of approved policy and land use plans.

Numerous authors have called for more imaginative, more
realistiic and less restrictive planning policies with respec
to retail location (see, for example, Davies, 1978; Dawson
and Kirby, 1980; Guy, 1980). However, it is probably fair
to say that such calls either fall on deaf ears, do not reach
the intended audience, or, if they do, they then take a
considerable time to be absorbed. A number of important
planning issues having various implications for retailing
are likely to arise in the years ahead.

110

The nature of planning intervention   The first relates to
government policies concerning planning intervention. Since
the election of a Conservative government in 1979 there have
been various initiatives to remove both government interference
in the operation of the private sector and public competition
with the private sector. This has resulted in government
selling off some of its holdings or repealing Acts of
Parliament. One of these affecting retailing was the Community
Land Act; through its provisions the government had earlier
sought to control and tax excessive financial gains made by
property transfer or development, although in reality one of
the Act's major effects was to suppress development. The
question arises, will the government extend its pro free
market stance to the provisions of the Town and Country
Planning Act, since it is here that the restrictive policy
against out-of-town shopping centres is operated. At present
there are no signs of a new and less interventionist Act; and
as there have been no new policy notes to local authorities
since the mid 1970s (Department of the Environment, 1977a),
little change can be expected in how local authorities use
the Act to prevent such centres.

Assuming the government retains the present Town and Country
Planning Act, the question then arises as to how government
intervention in planning will be modified to take better
account of retail innovation such as the out-of-town shopping
centre. Guy (1980) has argued that a degree of planning
intervention is necessary to improve the performance of the
market, to provide facilities that are beyond the scope of
the private sector alone and to prevent certain negative
externalities resulting from developments. However Guy
maintains that consideration of negative externatilities is
far from consistent; they receive much greater consideration
in the case of out-of-town centre development. In spite of
government protestations to the contrary, planning intervention
has worked in favour of certain interests over others,
interfered with normal market operations and restricted the
degree of shopping choice on the part of the consumer.

Development control   In the absence of a less interventionist
stance and since greater encouragement from central government
for out-of-town centres is not forthcoming, it will continue
to be through development control procedures that such centres
will come about. The private entrepreneur will have to be
prepared perhaps for a long and costly battle in order to
win local acceptance, or will have to exploit the weak points
in the system (i.e. go where the chances of acceptance are
greatest), resulting in a continuing uneven distribution of
out-of-town centres. The stakes seem so poor that many
entrepreneurs do not engage in a fight. Lee and Roberts
(1981), in a third study of planning appeals, note that few
planning refusals get to this stage; and even when they do,
there is only a small success rate, although this rate did
improve in the late 1970s. At this stage there is now a
greater recognition of the out-of-town centre as a community
function, less need to justify such a development and it is
not presumed to introduce adverse effects on existing
shopping centres. However, other aspects of land use remain

central issues and it is likely that out-of-town centres
will continue to be refused by the Secretary of State for
the Environment on the grounds especially of conflict with
green belt policies and intrusion into the countryside.

The inherent negativism of development control has forced
entrepreneurs to co-operate with local authorities so that
innovative features of retailing are incorporated with the
latter's development proposals (Jones, P.M., 1982). The
superstore and hypermarket phenomena, for example, have
become more acceptable as entrepreneurs have adapted their
proposals to fit in with local plans for district centres.
The danger here, and this will be looked at later, is that
co-operation may become synonymous with second best.

Structure Plans Structure planning at the county and
metropolitan county level sets out the policies to be adopted
with respect to out-of-town centres and in turn to decisions
that are likely to be given should a planning application
be received. (One assumes that local authorities would not
initiate their own out-of-town centres.) From the point of
view of innovative policies in retailing, structure plans
present a depressing spectacle. For the most part, local
authorities choose to interpret central government policy
(from policy notes and appeal decisions) as being negative
towards any development that is likely to alter significantly
the present retail hierarchy; although this may be done in
order to legitimise the structure plan authority's own retail
policies. Gibbs (1982), in a study of retail warehouses
(and other off-centre retail activities, since many local
authorities do not differentiate by type), analysed the
policies adopted in structure plans. A typology of different
policy decisions was formulated ranging from negative through
conservative to positive. Only a minority of authorities
are seen to be positive, and even here acceptance is based
on a number of criteria being satisfied which may give
generous scope for still being conservative. What is perhaps
most depressing at present is the inability of many local
authorities to differentiate the impact and demands, and
therefore the policies needed, between the various types of
out-of-town or off-centre retailing (for example, retail
warehouses, which are principally for non-convenience goods,
superstores and larger shopping centres).

Gibbs (1982) found that local authorities in Northern England
still tend to be more positive towards out-of-town or off-
centre retailing compared to authorities in the Midlands and
the South; also, later structure plans, as well as local
plans and other local retail policies, tend to be more
positive than earlier ones. These variations reflect multiple
-firm geographic origins and their diffusion and the greater
acceptance that comes with time and experience.

In the future it is likely that structure plans will be
modified as more liberal policies are adopted at the local
level, as development control and planning appeals work in
the entrepreneur's favour (and more off-centre retail
activities are developed) and as local authorities fill in

112

the void left by central government. However, local
authorities will increasingly differentiate between different
types of retail activity in off-centre locations. It can be
seen already that retail warehouses are more acceptable than
superstores and hypermarkets; the former are smaller and less
likely to affect existing retail centres, sell goods which
are more suited to warehouse than shop premises, and because
of the need for car parking and car pick up, are more suited
to off-centre than town or district centre locations. On the
other hand, out-of-town shopping centres of the Brent Cross
type will still be such a threat on parts of the existing
retail structure, that the few proposals likely to come
forward in the next twenty years or so will no doubt be
received with the same degree of horror as they have in the
past.

In spite of liberalising tendencies noted above, the same
incredible checklist of criteria to be satisfied at the
development control level can still be seen in the structure
plans, and therefore retail innovation will be a slow process.
The emphases within this list will wax and wane as the years
go by, varying from one local authority to the next and from
one planning inspector to the next, depending on the strength
of local protest and the degree to which central government
feels it should intervene. This checklist includes the
various land use considerations on the urban fringe (green
belt, agricultural land, community separation), traffic and
access problems, harmful effects on residential and
industrial land uses, bias in favour of certain consumer
groups over others and especially the impact on existing
retail centres. Existing centres, and in particular town
centres, are still regarded as sacrosanct; but in the
protection of past public investment and wider community
ideals, the government will continue to interfere with retail
competition and consumer choice, and, as will be seen below,
will hamper innovations in retail organisation and the
resulting changes in the retail hierarchy and retail location.
As in the past, government attitudes and policies will hamper
development, not restrict it altogether, since to do the
latter would be tantamount to telling people to return to
the lifestyle of a bygone era. Meanwhile, the government's
over cautious approach is costly, long winded and frustrating
for most concerned and has the stamp of futility writ large
across it.

7.3 CHANGES IN RETAIL ORGANISATION

It can be argued that it is difficult for government to
formulate policy when it is unclear how retailing will change
in the future. However, it is possible to discern various
trends, both within Britain and without, that government
could at least be responding to better than it has. Moreover,
if retail policies were more flexible, future innovations
could be more easily accommodated. A clash between the
entrepreneur and the government has been and will continue
to be, inevitable as long as the latter is wedded to
traditional shopping ways. (Changing retail organisation is
a reflection of 1) competition within the industry to attract

the consumer, bringing in its wake various economies of scale
and new techniques to reduce prices and 2) the creation of
a shopping environment which better fits consumers needs (or
perceived needs); increasingly, these changes may not be
easily accommodated within the existing retail structure.

First, the decline in the number of retail stores will
continue in response to the growth of multiple firms,
rationalisation within the industry and changing consumer
demands. It is difficult to predict how great that change
will be; an official attempt made in early 1970s underestimated
the extent of the decline by 1980 (National Economic Development
Office, 1971; see table 2.1). The replacement of the ten year
Census of Distribution by annual estimates will perhaps aid
in following national trends in the different retail sectors.

This decline reflects intra-industry competition; for example,
the take over of one multiple firm by another and the closing
down of superfluous stores (e.g. the Boots take over of
Timothy Whites). Within the one firm there continues to be
the replacement of smaller stores by a fewer number of larger
stores and or the geographic spread of the firm forcing
rationalisation upon others. Most of the major supermarket
chains, for example, still have a large number of older and
smaller stores which may become vulnerable in the light of
their own or other firm's plans. The development of
superstores has resulted in both new functions being included
in the store and the expansion of existing supermarket
functions, in turn threatening the viability of smaller,
often independently operated, stores.

As in the past, the growth of stores catering for new retail
functions or located in new residential areas or expanded
town centres will not make up for the loss of existing stores.
In addition to the loss through rationalisation and functional
change, the decline of population in inter-war, even post-war,
residential areas and the unsuitability of some of the stores
in these areas for modern retailing methods are resulting in
further losses.

Changes are taking place in retail organisation which result
in individuals or firms having to look beyond the traditional
shop or shopping centre. In fairness it must be stated that
at times little information concerning these changes is
readily available for planners and politicians to be aware of
what is going on and how to respond to it: they believe that
the existing retail structure can easily adapt or cope, and
it is often genuine ignorance, as much as outright
protectionism, that will lead to conflict at the development
control level. How changes in retail organisation influence
the retail hierarchy and retail location will be viewed in
7.4 and 7.5 below. At this point it is opportune to look at
the types of organisational change that are likely to occur.
In addition to larger and fewer stores and retail firms
undertaking more retail functions, innovations are taking
place in 1) the combination of functions undertaken in the
store; 2) how the goods are stored, displayed, sold and
taken home; 3) the size and design of both the store and

the site and 4) the general and specific locations that
entrepreneurs desire.

In the last ten years there has been a rapid increase in the
number of retail warehouses selling various combinations of
non-food items (Gibbs, 1981; 1982; Jones, P., 1982a; 1982b).
The most common are Do-it-Yourself (D.I.Y.) and home
improvement (which can include a wide range of building
materials, house fittings, paint and wallpaper, hardware and
electrical items), electrical goods and appliances, furniture
and carpets and car accessories. Many retail outlets do not
constitute a conventional shop or warehouse. The petrol
filling station is being modified to sell a range of
convenience items and car accessories instead of simply
selling petrol and repairing cars, and its car showroom may
even sell non-car oriented products; both of these changes of
use require permission under the Town and Country Planning
Act. Likewise, many builders' yards and other trade premises
and wholesale warehouse operations which normally do not sell
directly to the consumer, are engaging in retail operations
without approval under the Town and Country Planning Act.
(An order to desist, and perhaps a subsequent planning appeal
against the order, may await a complaint from the public or
a chance inspection.) In the last few years there has been
an explosion of garden centres in Britain. However, many are
no longer simply selling plants and seeds; they also include
exotic indoor plants, chemicals and fertilizers, garden and
patio furniture, garages and sheds and a host of other
hardware items. Many of the goods sold may go beyond the
original planning permission.

Recently, there has been an increase in the multi-functional
centre proposals of which retailing is only a part. Unlike
the earlier town and district centre developments of retail,
office and community service functions, these new proposals
are combining retailing (both speciality shops and superstores)
with different functions. The Asda superstore at North
Tilbury, for example, has been developed on Port of London
Authority land and will be associated with new housing,
transport facilities, industry and warehousing in a 'to be
improved' floodplain area (Ridgeway, 1981). A similar
development on the Park Royal Industrial Estate in West
London is intended to aid a declining industrial area,
problems of female labour recruitment and a dearth of local
shopping. In Birmingham a superstore has been built in
association with improvements to the Aston Villa football
club; and in Colchester developers for a second time have
offered the Colchester United football club a new and virtually
free stadium in return for planning permission for shops,
offices, industry and a sports complex. (An earlier proposal
was turned down on environmental and retail impact grounds.)

These new forms of retail development do not fit well into
the traditional shop. Often large display and storage areas
are needed, and in the case of garden centres these are
possible (an cheaper) in the open air. The converted factory,
warehouse or garage are more suitable, although increasingly
a purpose-built facility is desired. Since 10 000 to 15 000

115

sq.ft. of net space is generally needed on one floor, plus
adjacent surface car parking, most traditional shopping
centres are considered to be unsuitable. Moreover, the
emphasis is on discount prices and reducing overheads, and
therefore, the very functional, windowless building would be
aesthetically unsuitable for the average shopping centre
facade. There is also an increasing emphasis on cash and
carry. Given the bulky and or heavy nature of items such as
self-assembled furniture, lengths of wood, carpets or boxes
of bathroom tiles, there is little likelihood of these being
carried to the bus stop (or if you did, of then being allowed
on the bus!), and thus it makes nonsense of planners' demands
for proximity of public transport Indeed, greater
consideration has to be given to site layouts where there
can be easily accessible car pick-up areas in addition to
adequate nearby car parking.

7.4 THE CHANGING RETAIL HIERARCHY

The wider forces of change and changing retail organisation
will continue to place pressure on the traditional retail
hierarchy at both the inter- and intra-urban levels. The
effect of larger and fewer' will undoubtedly be to enhance
the relative importance of some retail centres and to decrease
that of others; fewer large superstores in an area not
increasing in population will spatially extend the catchment
area of a certain centre, or increase the consumer draw, at
some other centre's expense. This development is further
enhanced by improved consumer mobility and an increasing
demand for sophisticated, higher-order shopping involving
more lengthy journeys.

At the inter-urban level the larger town is seemingly
favoured over the smaller one. However, the congestion and
inconvenience associated with car travel and parking in
central areas and the increasing uniformity, blandness, even
mediocrity, from one chain store dominated High Street to the
next, may account for the increasing vitality of so many
smaller market towns and overgrown villages, especially in
middle class areas, with their greater predominance of small
independently operated quality shops. This virtually depends
largely on a walking population within the town and car travel
often over an extensive rural area. Also, many of these
smaller towns are becoming greater tourist attractions and
in their wake are coming improved hotel and restaurant
facilities, art and crafts and antique shops and other small
scale tourist facilities.

While there may have been a decline in town centre retail
growth since the mid 1970s, the continuing importance of the
larger town at the inter-urban level has been promoted through
its suburban or district centre shopping initiatives. Urban
fringe superstores and retail warehouses are often more
conveniently placed to the car-owning, smaller town and rural
resident some distance away than to the public transport user
within the town. Numerous impact studies show the superstore
to have far more than a local residential draw: indeed one
could say that it would have to in order to be viable. In the

case of the Tesco superstore in the High Woods, Colchester district centre the developers are only just beginning the new residential area surrounding it; the store at present relies entirely on other residential areas and neighbouring towns and villages, and thus taking trade away from existing centres.

Improved mobility by motorways and trunk roads and the attractive features of new, purpose built, multi-functional facilities pose some interesting challenges to the public and private sector and the possibilities of a major divergence from the existing inter-urban retail hierarchy. At present the major multiple firms are loyal and financially wedded to the traditional hierarchy and have shown little interest in out-of-town centres: the consumer, prodded by a loyal local press, has for the most part behaved likewise. But will this loyalty survive? The signs are already there that it may not. More multiple firms are showing interest in out-of-town and off-centre developments; this is often encouraged by the advent of new developers proposing new multi-functional activities (and the prospects of a declining market share for existing developers), consumers voting with their feet (or their cars) and the prospect of less public financing (and therefore worsening infrastructure) of town and district centre development.

The experience of Brent Cross and the memories of what could have been at Haydock Park will continue to promote interest in other large out-of-town centres. The 'soon to be completed' M25 London Orbital Motorway, for example, has encouraged flurries of activity in business circles concerning its influence on existing centres and the possibilities of new centres. Baden and Jones (1983) estimate that 4.5 million people will live within ten minutes drive time of the M25; and assuming a durable expenditure growth at the average rate (constant prices) for the last ten years with no improved turnover performance of existing floorspace, there is the potential for an additional 25 million sq.ft. gross floorspace in the next twenty years. Given local authority preference for development in existing centres, Baden and Jones suggest there would not be scope for more than five out-of-town centres of up to 1 million sq.ft. gross each. However, given the considerable underrepresentation of superstores and hypermarkets in the Greater London area, compared to other parts of the country, it is probably in this field that significant development may arise. With or without new centre development, the M25 is likely to enhance competition between certain existing centres to the detriment of those which are perceived to be less attractive.

The smaller out-of-town centre, dominated by a superstore or hypermarket, could become a more important node in the inter-urban retail hierarchy, thereby creating further pressures for development. The Calcott, Reading SavaCentre, for example, is more than a hypermarket serving parts of Berkshire, Hampshire, Oxfordshire and Buckinghamshire: its location adjacent to an M4 Motorway junction and approximately equidistant between M4 service centres has resulted in the

SavaCentre becoming another service centre, with cheaper
petrol, pleasant eating facilities and the added bonus of
shopping. To what extent will this out-of-town centre act
as a catalyst for other retail development, which if it is
approved, would throw a further wrench into the Central
Berkshire Structure Plan? (Berkshire County Council, 1980).

At the intra-urban level it can be seen that the traditional
three or four level retail hierarchy is not operating, and
cannot operate, as planners and politicians intend. First,
there is still an incredible reluctance to see retail trade
diverted away from the town centre. This does not mean just
durable-good trade: many local authorities want to retain
the bulk of convenience-good trade in the town centre as
well. In an age of the superstore, bulk buying and car use,
untold pressures are still being put on town centres. The
infrastructure often cannot cope with such pressures. Yet
to put in improved roads and car parking, for example, could
be costly, and when finally built damaging to the urban
fabric and aesthetic appeal; and all this could ultimately
result in diverting traffic to another centre. Little or no
study has been done on just how much floorspace a town centre
can bear before it becomes socially and economically more
desirable to locate that space elsewhere. The dictum that
local authorities too often use is: all additional retail
space is welcome in the town centre, providing there is a
need (and this may not be too closely scrutinised); the
infrastructure will be improved accordingly, although not
necessarily at the same time.

Second, the overloading of the town centre has meant that
district centres perform perhaps an emasculated role. Too
many continue to be a large collection of small shops, lacking
superstores or large supermarkets and concentrating on
convenience rather than durable goods. The intention is that
they fulfil the everyday needs of the surrounding population
and not compete with the town centre, although these needs
may be far from satisfied. As the other extreme, many new
district centres dominated by a superstore and perhaps
including a range of other stores fulfil far more than
everyday local needs; they have extensive catchment areas,
promoting less frequent, one-stop bulk buying and competing
readily with many established centres.

Third, the neighbourhood centre will continue to have an
important role to play especially from the point of view of
convenience, although this convenience is invariably set
against higher prices compared to other centres. This has
resulted in the neighbourhood centre performing a smaller
proportion of one's convenience-good needs; and the small
supermarkets especially, unable to compete with the superstore
elsewhere, are closing or adapting. The exact performance
of a centre is difficult to predict, since it will depend not
just on the size and nature of its catchment area population
and its location with respect to other centres, but on the
developments that will take place in those other centres.

Smaller groupings of shops at the fourth level tend to be
discouraged since they do not offer an adequate range of
convenience functions. However, there is increasing pressure
for a single shop or group of shops, divorced from the other
three levels of the hierarchy. We are no longer talking
about the corner store or a parade of four shops, but the
suburban retail warehouse or out-of-town superstore. There
is an increasing demand for retail space which cannot fit
the traditional hierarchy in terms of location, size of unit,
function and catchment area. The district/out-of-town centre
superstore has already set the scene, and its diffusion is
by no means universal; the retail warehouse is as yet in its
infancy; and the possibilities for the multi-functional centre,
outside of the town centre, are endless.

In spite of the formulations of structure plans we can see
that the traditional hierarchy is not sancrosanct, and to
quote Dawson and Kirby (1980, 99), "no longer is it reasonable
to think of a nice tidy hierarchy of centre provision".

7.5 CHANGING RETAIL LOCATION

Changes that are taking place in retail organisation and
consumer behaviour are not only leading to a breakdown in
the traditional retail hierarchy, but also where retail
operations are located. There will continue to be pressure
for out-of-town or at least off-centre within town, locations
for a number of reasons.

The traditional intra-urban hierarchy saw retail location
closely associated with residential location at the district
and neighbourhood levels, with an accompanying emphasis on
walking to shop. However, entrepreneurs are increasingly
less interested in these facets of retailing. The nature of
the product sold and or the bulk or weight that would have
to be carried home virtually preclude anything other than
car travel. Furthermore, the size of the operation is often
such that it takes a larger residential area, thus beyond the
limits of walking, to make the operation economically viable.
Entrepreneurs now feel more free to seek unconventional
locations, such as 'green field' sites on the urban fringe
or in an industrial estate, the conversion of industrial and
warehouse premises in inner and outer city areas, or the
cleared or vacant site within the urban area. But it is
these locations that interfere with planners' concepts of a
retail hierarchy and the need to segregate urban functions:
indeed it is thought by planners that too much time and
effort have been spent since the Second World War organising
this segregation to want to return to the entrepreneurial
freedom of a bygone era.

It can be seen in 7.3 that changing retail organisation is
bringing about increasing demands for new retail locations.
The present experience of retail warehouses (see, for example,
Gibbs, 1981; 1982) shows the clash between traditional and
innovative thinking on retail location. Planners and
politicians still desire to have retail warehouses closely
associated with existing shopping centres, albeit perhaps on

the fringe of these centres. However, from the point of
view of land and building costs, vehicular access, goods and
pick-up and parking, sites outside existing centres are being
sought. Also, the amount of land or size of building required
for a retail warehouse and the design of the building make
for an uneasy addition to an existing shopping centre; we
must come to terms with the fact that not all retailing can
be accomplished from the traditional shop. In would be
preferable for planners to incorporate various new locations
for retail warehouses in local plans, rather than stick to
their guns and face possible defeat via the development
control process. To plan ahead rather than afterwards also
has the advantage of possibly avoiding the second best
syndrome, i.e. entrepreneurs seeking locations where they
are more likely to receive planning permission rather than
locations that are better for entrepreneurs and consumers
alike.

Much enthusiasm in both business and planning circles has
resulted from the co-operation that is now taking place
between entrepreneurs and local authorities in building
superstores in district centres; indeed, entrepreneurs are
persuading local authorities that superstores can stand alone
rather than be located alongside smaller shops. However,
this co-operation is often done in the knowledge that planning
permission will not be forthcoming for an out-of-town location
and the possibility of a reversal at the planning appeal
stage has to be matched against high legal costs, delay and
lost store income.

The co-operation between entrepreneurs and local authorities
is not necessarily in the best interests of consumers and the
community at large. The monopolistic practice of the
superstore, if it is the sole store, now seems a far off
1970s problem, long since forgotten in the realisation that
either mobility has improved for consumers to patronise other
stores or consumers can still use small local shops. The chief
problem underlying this co-operation is that entrepreneurs
are often accepting inferior locations.

The planned district centre is not merely associated with new
residential development but is still located in the heart of
it. The centre is designed in terms of a hierarchy of local
roads, and even cycle and pedestrian routes, as if it is only
to be used by that residential development; and since it is
not, then traffic from outside will ultimately bring extra
hazards upon the local area. A comparison of the two
superstore developments in the Reading area illustrate
important locational variations and the inferior location of
one of them. The SavaCentre at Calcott, which was refused
local planning permission, is in a highly visable and easily
accessible location on the A4 road, adjacent to an M4 junction
to the west of Reading; it is close to, but not an integral
part of, a number of new and long established residential
areas and served by a number of inter and intra-urban bus
routes. On the other hand, the Asda, Lower Earley superstore
to the south east of Reading is a planned district centre to
serve what will become the largest single private housing

development in Europe. But since the store also draws
consumers from other areas, it would seem logical to have
chosen an equally good location on the edge of this development
and in close proximity to the M4 and 'A' roads. Instead,
the Asda superstore is in the centre of the development, well
away from the 'A' roads, let alone an M4 junction, approached
by a myriad of poorly signposted, residential streets and
displaying all the various conflicts between retail and non-
retail movements.

Poor locational decisions have a habit of coming back to
haunt one, and the results are there which even the layman
cannot fail to observe. Building parades of shops at
important urban road junctions in the 1930s can be appreciated
in an age when car ownership was the luxury of a small
minority; but building superstores at similar locations in
the late 1970s would seem totally irresponsible. Yet there
are many examples of this poor site use. In Colchester, for
example, in the aftermath of the numerous refusals for out-
of-town centres on the western fringe of the town (Department
of the Environment, 1977b), one of the affected firms
(Sainsbury's) received planning permission in 1978 for a
superstore in a nearby decaying neighbourhood centre. The
site is small and the ratio of car-parking spaces to sales
area is far too low for a middle class area where second car
ownership is higher than average. Furthermore, the store is
situated cheek-by-jowl with the pavement at a traffic light
controlled junction on an 'A' road; and both queuing for the
car park and the exit from it result in traffic chaos at peak
times. Sufficient consumer dissatisfaction has arisen for
Sainsbury's and the local authority in 1983 to be thinking
of a new location. However, if planners had done their
homework properly, this expensive mistake, and many like it,
could have been averted. But it is feared that in the rush
for approval (in order perhaps to stay ahead of, or catch up
with, competitors) entrepreneurs are prepared to go for less
than desirable sites; and local authorities, in the absence
of good retail locational guidelines and little intervention
from above, simply compound the errors.

It is paramount in the years ahead that more consideration
be given by government to the finer points of retail location.
There is certainly no lack of manuals on the subject, but
Guy (1980, 55) notes that under conditions of uncertainty
and through pressures of time entrepreneurs have not
adopted the best methods of locational assessment. Also, one
might add, this is not helped by a public sector that is
insensitive to the needs of the car-using consumer and the
desires of entrepreneurs in satisfying them.

7.6 CONCLUSION

In the years ahead it can be seen that various changes taking
place in British society which have relevance for retailing
and consumer behaviour will result in continued pressure for
retailing in out-of-town and off-centre locations. On the
other hand, it seems that government will continue to be slow

to recognise and embrace such innovations, believing that
the changes taking place in retail organisation can be
contained within the existing retail hierarchy and in
traditional locations to the benefit of all. Clearly, this
is not to the benefit of 1) a growing sector of British
society, who do not shop in traditional fashion, and 2)
those entrepreneurs whose retail outlets do not fit into
the traditional shopping centre. Conservatism and
protectionism on the part of government will continue to
lead to conflict, lost opportunities, poor planning
decisions, inefficiencies and unnecessary consumer costs.

8. Summary and conclusions

During the past fifteen years the out-of-town shopping centre has been the subject of a quite emotive debate involving existing retailers, local politicians, the development industry and academic and professional groups and individuals. As is common in such debates, claims and counterclaims can become very polarised, and both sides tend to draw upon an extensive list of arguments (at times somewhat remotely connected with retailing) to back up·their claims. All too often this exercise has been allowed to mask the more substantive case for accepting, or not accepting, out-of-town centres. The present study has attempted to identify the major factors which underlie the general opposition towards out-of-town centres, the conflict situations that such centres cause and the problems associated with trying to accommodate retail innovations such as this into the existing retail framework. The following themes were identified in order to understand the overall problem:

Changing retail structure   All too often the out-of-town centre has been viewed in isolation from other elements of the retail structure. Whilst it does constitute a major departure in some aspects (certain locational characteristics, design, land and property management and store hinterlands), in others it is part of a continuum of change that has been affecting retailing in Britain, especially since the Second World War. This change has included a considerable decrease in the total number of shops and an increase in the size of establishments and the proportion of trade undertaken by multiple stores; the trend to fewer and larger stores continues as the multiple firms themselves rationalise their operations. A significant part of this organisational shift has been the development of the supermarket and its expansion into the superstore and hypermarket as more and more products are made available under the one roof. Whilst the bulk of this development has taken place in traditional centres, especially town centres, entrepreneurs have attempted to seek out locations which provide them with cheaper building and operating costs and their customers with greater convenience. A far smaller trend in Britain has been the development of comparison-goods shopping away from traditional centres; as yet only one large private, free-standing regional shopping centre exists, although there are a number of smaller developments which qualify on the basis of the type of product sold.

123

The development of the out-of-town centre undoubtedly will
influence the existing retail hierarchy in both the inter
and intra-urban context. (However, it is not fully
appreciated that the retail hierarchy is undergoing change
irrespective of whether out-of-town centres are being
developed; and where it is appreciated, change within the
existing hierarchy is preferred since it is thought to offer
less chance of serious competition and to maintain community
values and financial investment.)

Out-of-town centre impact   In considering the out-of-town
centre problem it can be seen that the nature of the impact
of these centres on the existing inter and intra-urban retail
hierarchy is far from well understood. Whilst numerous impact
studies have been undertaken, the dissemination of their
results into some of the areas where it matters has not
always taken place, or at least not taken place well. This
in part reflects their piecemeal coverage and emphasis on
local (even hypothetical) conditions, but also the lack of
good vehicles of communication to make the valid generalisation
better known. Moreover, it may be difficult to differentiate
the effects of an out-of-town centre from other developments
taking place within the existing retail hierarchy. Generally
the impact of an out-of-town centre extends over a wider area
than a traditional centre of equivalent size, and it is
selective in terms of which stores and centres it may take
trade away from. However, those who oppose out-of-town
centres most vigorously (e.g. independent retailers in nearby
centres) are invariably not those who stand to lose the most,
although apart from some notable exeptions, the out-of-town
centre has not resulted in any disastrous effects on the
existing retail structure; and many would argue that the
effects that have arisen (like any other readjustments in the
retail hierarchy) are only private enterprise working at its
best, creating ultimately an economically more efficient
system for both retailer and consumer alike.

It is claimed that the impact of out-of-town centres on
consumers is far from universal and only some benefit from
their development; but whilst this is true, it is debateable
whether this should be used as a means of preventing those
who would use such a centre from having the opportunity to
do so. Besides, the private sector in the past has never
had to guarantee universality in the availability of
opportunities before receiving permission from a public body.
Rather than oppose because not all can benefit, it might be
more productive in the long run to encourage all those who
want to be able to reach such a retail opportunity. There
is no doubt that the many attractive features amongst out-of-
town centres have widened consumer awareness and preference;
these include lower prices, the convenience of location and
accessibility, and the overall shopping environment.

Conflict on the rural-urban fringe   Unlike many other types
of retail activity, the out-of-town centre presents a major
challenge to well entrenched views concerning the rural-urban
fringe, and many features of the centre, including its relative
location, visibility and design, traffic and car parking and

124

other service needs are given close scrutiny when planning applications are made. Compared to many other countries, it is perhaps to Britain's credit that there are such rigid and well observed policies to protect the countryside and rural amenity. On the other hand, it can be argued that the policy could be amended to channel growth areas and retain rural areas in a different form that would enhance circulation patterns, and second to encourage in decentralisation a better distribution of urban activities than currently exists. The out-of-town centre is part of this decentralisation and would bring better retail services closer to new residential growth. However, this aspect about an out-of-town centre is lost or played down in the wave of preservation of the countryside that invariably ensues. In the operation of land use planning there is little allowance for compromise or the effective working of both urban and rural land uses; it is more a question of how an urban oriented proposal can 'chip away' or circumvent rural based policies.

There are many bases on which an out-of-town centre can be opposed, including divergence from the existing or proposed land use plan, an extension of the built-up area, the preservation of agricultural land and green belt areas and development in isolated or 'green field' locations. It is usually not too difficult to find one or more of these to use as a basis for objecting to an out-of-town centre; but in an area which rests on the dictates of development control, it is not surprising to find a lack of consistency at both local and central government levels in what constitutes an objection.

Resistance to retail change   The strongest opposition to out-of-town centres emanates from the local level from the time that an entrepreneur is considering development through to the submission and deliberation on an actual planning application. It is usually argued by opponents that additional retail facilities are not needed (either in total or in that location), or if they are needed, to allow them in an out-of-town centre would constitute too damaging a prospect in terms of the existing retail hierarchy. While there are valid arguments against overprovision or damaging the existing hierarchy, it is necessary to examine carefully the nature of the argument and also who is making it. Opponents tend to be local government professional staff, small businessmen and local politicians, and many local politicians can be small businessmen or have strong allegiances in that camp. This raises the cry that in objecting to out-of-town centres many of these people may be attempting to protect a vested interest in terms of personal or public financial investment. Much of the protectionism may by misguided because the nature of the impact on the existing retail hierarchy may be assessed more seriously than would actually happen, although by knowingly exaggerating it might better convince the decision makers to oppose an application. A more serious aspect is that the planning process favours such opponents. For it is the opponents in many instances who become the juries. Also, the nature of the evidence that is considered in local planning deliberations and planning inquiries tends to be limited and focusses on the negative aspects of what would happen if the individual out-of-town centre is built, rather than overall shopping policies and the benefits to be gained by such development.

The charge or overprovision of retail facilities is hardly convincing. Since it has been allowed, often generously, within the existing retail hierarchy, the argument could be seen as another form of protectionism. Some overprovision is necessary in facilitating technological improvements, competitive rents and better locational choices, all of which help to contribute to a more efficient retail environment. Much of the protectionism that is evident relates not to the individual retailer and his livelihood (since land use planning cannot be seen to be used to prevent competition between retailers and retail methods) but to the existing retail hierarchy, in particular the redevelopment that has taken place in town centres. Again, with little recourse to the many impact studies and drawing too readily on North American examples, there is a fear that the out-of-town centre will jeopardise retailing in town centres and in turn lead to a faltering of the town centre economy and further social, economic, physical and planning problems. Nowhere at this local level are there really any serious doubts raised about continuing the promotion of the existing retail hierarchy.

<u>Government policy and planning</u> The present status of the out-of-town shopping centre in Britain reflects a situation where the central government has always been weakly involved in retail matters. Ministerial policy has done little to defuse local resistance; the emphasis has been the promotion of the status quo, especially town centre redevelopment, with a cautionary stance taken regarding out-of-town centres. Instead of an overall retail policy and firm directives to local authorities to plan for such eventualities, the government has favoured, somewhat belatedly, ambiguous guidelines which are supposed to help local planning authorities in development control matters if and when the problem arises. Changes to the Town and Country Planning and Local Government Acts have improved the decision-making process, but it falls short of what is necessary, especially in the adoption of regional strategies for retailing and overcoming local prejudices.

The emphasis on development control rather than on overall retail policy effectively places decision making at the local level. But since the greatest amount of opposition is to be found here, it is scarcely surprising that so few out-of-town centres have been approved. In the absence of strong central government policy it is left to county and metropolitan county authorities in their structure plans to decide upon strategies for retail development in their respective areas. In general, if any mention is made of out-of-town shopping centres, the tendency is to be opposed, emphasising the strengths of the existing retail structure and the damage that could be done by the developing outside of this. To continue with the present development control approach not only means an erratic distribution of out-of-town centres, but the possibility that

126

the locations that are approved are less than optimal
(simply the least line of resistance by a developer in the
context of local uncertainty), while many of the locations
that are rejected could in a different political climate
have provided such optimal conditions.

Prospects for the 1980s and beyond A final chapter undertook
the difficult task of looking at the future retail climate.
There is little doubt that the many broader changes in our
society, which have some influence on retailing and consumer
behaviour, will result in a continuing pressure for out-of-
town, or at least off-centre within town, locations. A
favourable response from government will continue to be slow.
Most initiatives will come from the local level, and will be
through development control procedures rather than an *a priori*
policy favouring out-of-town centres and setting out possible
locations. Most local authorities will no doubt remain
opposed to out-of-town centres for many years to come; but
the experiences gained from those out-of-town centres which
have developed are resulting in various liberalising tendencies
in recent Structure and Local Plans and in planning appeal
reports.

The need to be flexible in the public sector reflects various
changes taking place in retail organisation that mitigate
against a rigid adherence to the existing retail hierarchy
and retail locations. Changes in site and building designs,
consumer travel needs, selling and storage methods and multi-
functional organisations (e.g. shopping associated with
football stadia, dockland redevelopment or industrial
development) may make nonsense of policies designed to contain
retailing in town and district centres. Attempts to weld
out-of-town centres with the traditional district centre, for
example, can be seen as a compromise; it may not be entirely
what developers want, but it can assuage the worst of local
fears. However, it should be seen as going for second best.
Developers would do everyone concerned a favour by lobbying
hard for their first choice. The retail hierarchy at the
inter or intra-urban level is not sacrosanct and retail
locations must take account of increasing car useage and
greater convenience for the car shopper.

From a study of retail innovation and the out-of-town shopping
centre in Britain it is possible to highlight some concerns
for further consideration by government, the retail industry
and the academic and professional areas:

The need for better communication An important aspect of
local resistance to out-of-town shopping centres is the
overreaction in terms of their likely impact on existing
retail facilities. Deliberate overreaction can pay off in
getting some competitive proposal squashed, but much of it
is genuine and relates to poor diffusion of research on the
topic. Central government may judge that enough is known
for local government to make adequate decisions and a call-in
policy is only needed in certain circumstances. But it can
be seen that local government and its officers do not always

have a sufficient comprehension of the research that has
been undertaken elsewhere, and when they do, are not always
able to use it to its best advantage. There is a need for
central government to be more communicative on this point,
by distilling this impact research and setting it out in
more detailed guidelines to local authorities and the retail
industry. This would help offset the tendency by existing
retailers to dramatise their argument by choosing those
studies which illustrate where the impact of an out-of-town
centre has been most serious.

The need for better policy   One must ask how adequate it is
i) to leave a question such as out-of-town shopping centres
so much in the hands of local government and then largely
as a development control matter for the occasion if and when
it arises; and ii) in handing the matter over to local
government, to accompany this with guidelines that are
ambiguous and stress the negative aspects on other land uses
and activities rather than include the positive aspects in
both the short and long term of developing out-of-town
centres. The fact that out-of-town centres have been approved
implies that central government condones their development,
and it behoves it to look upon their development in a more
comprehensive manner. Given the structure of local government
there is a need for adopting clearer structure plan strategies
to ensure a balanced distribution of retail opportunities
and to prevent, for example, needless municipal rivalry and
overprovision. Furthermore, with the loose structure of many
urban regions and sub-regions it could be more efficient to
promote the development of a well placed out-of-town centre,
rather than attempt to upgrade any one existing centre.
Central government could do more to ensure that out-of-town
centres are not conceived as retail lepers but better
incorporated into the traditional retail hierarchy. Centres
dominated by a superstore or hypermarket, for example, can
be viewed as new style district centres; and with better
co-operation between local government and the development
industry there could be greater possiblities of the former's
proposals for district centres reaching fruition via the
latter's initiatives, rather than the developer having to
give in to local government for the sake of obtaining planning
permission. The role of central government here would be the
directive to local authorities to consider such eventualities,
especially their location, in their structure planning, and
for central government to then adjudicate; where sub-regional,
comparison-goods centres such as Brent Cross are concerned
and a more regional approach is necessary, the matter (at
least initially) could be undertaken entirely by central
government.

The power of positive thinking   Better policy will only be
facilitated by adopting a more positive stance in terms of
out-of-town shopping development. This is not to say that
negative aspects and effects on other land uses and activities
should not be considered as a development control matter;
but these should be examined in the context of the best
location for an out-of-town/district centre offering the
least disruption, rather than be used simply to block

development because it is seen to offer too much competition. A more positive stance by central government is necessary if only to get in step with what consumers are already doing, if given a chance; and developers seem only too ready to provide. While it may be chic to scoff at big business antics, building money-making retail centres, undercutting the small businessman by slashing prices and pandering to mass consumer appeal and the car-owning public, there is no lack of consumers prepared to engage in such activity. Impact studies would indicate that the free-standing, privately sponsored out-of-town centre (and also its in-town counterpart, most likely a superstore in an existing retail centre) is no short term aberration. To oppose out-of-town shopping centres, simply because they may threaten the status quo and the consumers who depend on it, is to do a disservice to the consumers who would gain by them. Moreover, to use hypothetical studies to show that there is little consumer demand for such centres indicates a certain naivety about the extent to which consumers will modify their behaviour once the opportunity arises.

While government does not wish to be seen using land use planning to prevent competition between retailers and retail methods, to promote the negative aspects of out-of-town centres rather than the positive ones is to play into the hands of vested interests who want to protect the status quo. However, the one overriding difficulty in adopting a more positive stance is that the vested interests include not only the small businessman but government itself, at both the national and local levels, which over the years has made considerable investment of public monies in the existing retail structure. Government therefore has to convince itself perhaps that retailing is a commodity like anything else where investment strategy can, and must, change over time to suit new sets of circumstances with depreciation or no further investment in one area and new investment elsewhere. Meanwhile the opposition of the small businessman could be defused if better attempts were made by both government and large development interests to incorporate him more into out-of-town centre projects. The out-of-town centre, unlike existing retail centres, is viewed all too often as a monolith to big private corporations and national, multiple retail firms where the small businessman has no part.

Innovative versus traditional retail locations It is difficult to promote better policy and more positive thinking with respect to out-of-town centres when attitudes favouring the status quo are so entrenched in the decision-making body. In the interests of good physical and economic planning and social justice government has seen fit to allow the decentralisation of residential, industrial, commercial and various public land use activities but has balked at retail activities following suit. There is much hazy discussion about the results of such decentralisation in terms of lost investment, increasing physical blight, loss of confidence amongst the public, spillover effects in non-retail areas, the bad influence on the town's overall image and the not altogether too convincing a comparison with some North

American examples. But to restrict retail decentralisation contributes to a disequilibrium situation where for many consumers there is a greater or more inconvenient journey to shop than need be. And while government has restricted where consumers can shop, it has not done the same to the mode of transport they can use; the result is that the most restricted sites, such as town centres, have recently had to endure in the car the upsurge of the most land hungry and inefficient form of transport and the consequent expensive readjustments to the urban fabric. There is virtually no attempt to argue the case of innovative versus traditional retail locations in terms of cost effectiveness. Whilst our techniques of cost-benefit analysis are highly sophisticated there is a marked reluctance to use them here. Also, there is little incentive perhaps when government is so heavily involved in traditional developments.

The fear of innovative methods Government and the retail industry as a whole are very much aware, it can be argued, of the technological changes taking place in the retail sector and changing consumer demands and how both of these point to a need for a redistribution of retail activities. But there is a fear that in relaxing development control procedures or planning specifically for retail location change that the flood of proposals and resulting development in out-of-town centres would do irreparable harm to the existing order. However, irreparable harm would only take place if the existing retail structure attempted to compete where it was not possible rather than readjust and complement. Official thinking on retail matters fears change rather than learning to cope with it and ultimately promoting it. Much of the fear focusses on town centre retailing; but there is nothing to say that retailing there must remain in tact. Rather than the town centre remaining the sole, major comparison-goods (and even cheap convenience-goods) centre for a larger hinterland for all consumers, it can follow the North American example by divesting some of its roles on other centres closer to residential areas and concentrating on certain of its other functions, for example retailing for the daily office population, tourists and inner city residents and developing specialty retailing and various services which need a large hinterland to provide sufficient threshold or demand the closer proximity of other services. As yet, only very tenuous steps have been taken to release British town centres of their very dominant role in retailing.

The threat of a reversal Finally, much of the hesitancy over approving out-of-town shopping centres stems from belief that the circumstances which have led to their approval and development so far could be short lived, and that there could be a time in the not too distant future when circumstances are such that car-oriented, out-of-town shopping is no longer popular. This is a particularly luddite sentiment, and if in the past it had been extended to other areas of the economy, society would have progressed or changed very little. Indeed, there is little reason to single out one aspect of economic development for this type of treatment and could be indicative of opponents of out-of-town centres clinging to anything if it enables such centres to be rejected.

The underlying factor which fuels the doubts is the possibility of energy shortages, and thus the need for conservation, the declining use of the car and the subsequent retrenchment of those areas of the economy, land uses and activities that are dependent on the car. The out-of-town centre is therefore particularly vulnerable. But it could be argued that the vulnerability when extended across the entire economy would about qualify us for the complete collapse of organised society as we know it. It is more likely given present technological possibilities and consumer pressure that alternative energy sources and other types of personalised transport will fill the void. Other technological changes may require more infrequent shopping trips. Britain is some way behind other countries in the frequency that consumers purchase convenience goods. The move to larger packaging, more home storage space, increased freezer owner-ship and home computer base shopping decisions and saving time (for other activities) by more one-stop purchasing would contribute to such energy saving in the retail area. There is little reason to believe that the out-of-town centre would not play an even more important role, especially as the conventional small shop declined in favour of the larger, combined warehouse-retail structure.

The likelihood that the out-of-town centre may decline in popularity is further weakened by the arguments of many urban specialists, particularly in North America, that a more fully decentralised city is better in terms of energy efficiency than overly concentrating certain activities in central areas. It would be better to have consumers drive (but less frequently) to higher-order suburban retail locations rather than drive or use public transport for longer journeys to city centres.

The out-of-town shopping centre is a feature of the urban environment that in the long term will not be wished away easily. There is a strong need for decision makers to promote the benefits of such centres by planning for them in a more positive, forceful, informative and comprehensive fashion. In this way, an innovative feature, which has been granted a tenuous foothold and has proved popular with a large proportion of the shopping public with ready access to one, can be made more universally available and acceptable.

References

Baden, T. and Jones, R. 1983. M25 retail. *Planning News*, May.

Bennison, D.J. and Davies, R.L. 1981. The impact of town centre shopping schemes in Britain. *Progress in Planning*, 14(1).

Berkshire County Council, 1980. *Central Berkshire Structure Plan Written Statement*, (Berkshire County Council, Reading).

Berry, B.J.L. 1963. *Commercial structure and commercial blight*. Research Paper No. 85, (Department of Geography, University of Chicago, Chicago).

Berry, B.J.L. and Garrison, W.L. 1958a. A note on central place theory and the range of a good. *Economic Geography*, 34, 304-311.

Berry, B.J.L. and Garrison, W.L. 1958b. Recent developments of central place theory. *Papers and Proceedings of the Regional Science Association*, 4, 107-120.

Berry, B.J.L., Parsons, S.J. and Platt, R.H. 1968. *The impact of urban renewal on small business*. (University of Chicago, Center for Urban Studies, Chicago).

Blake, J. 1976. Brent Cross Shopping Centre. *Town and Country Planning*, 44, 231-236.

Blowers, A. 1980. *The limits of power: the politics of local planning policy*. (Pergamon, Oxford).

Board of Trade, 1964. *Report on the census of distribution and other services*. 1961, (H.M.S.O., London).

Burns, W. 1959. *British shopping centres*. (Leonard Hill, London).

Carol, H. 1960. The hierarchy of central functions within the city. *Annals, Association of American Geographers*, 50, 419-438.

Carruthers, W.I. 1962. Service centres in Greater London. *Town Planning Review*, 33, 5-31.

Carruthers, W.I. 1967. Major shopping centres in England and Wales 1961. *Regional Studies*, 1, 65-81.

Cassells, S.C. 1980. Retail competition and planning. *Retail and Distribution Management*, 8, Nov/Dec, 32-37.

Champion, A.G. 1978. Issues over land. in: Davies, R.L. and Hall, P. (eds.), *Issues in urban society*. (Penguin, Harmondsworth), 21-52.

City Of Oxford, 1954. *City of Oxford Development Plan*. (Oxford).

Cohen, S.B. 1961. Location research programming for voluntary food chains. *Economic Geography*, 37, 1-11.

Davies, R.L. 1976. *Marketing Geography*. (Retailing and Planning Associates, Corbridge, Northumberland).

Davies, R.L. 1977. A framework for commercial planning policies. *Town Planning Review*, 48, 42-58.

Davies, R.L. 1978. Issues in retailing. in: Davies, R.L. and Hall, P. (eds.), *Issues in urban society*, (Penguin, Harmondsworth), 132-160.

Davies, R.L. (ed.) 1979. *Retail planning in the European Community*. (Saxon House, Farnborough).

Davies, W.K.D. 1968. The need for replication in Human Geography: some central place examples. *Tijdschrift voor Economische en Social Gr*, 59, 145-155.

Daws, L.F. and Bruce, A.J. 1971. *Shopping in Watford*. (Building Research Station, Watford).

Dawson, J.A. 1979. *The marketing environment*. (Croom Helm, London).

Dawson, J.A. (ed.) 1980. *Retail geography*. (J. Wiley, New York).

Dawson, J.A. and Kirby, D.A. 1980. Urban retail provision and consumer behaviour: some examples from Western Society. in: Herbert, D.T. and Johnston, R.J. (eds.), *Geography and the urban environment, progress in research and applications*. (J. Wiley, Chichester), 3, 87-132.

Department of the Environment, 1965. *Haydock Park*. File No. APP/1186/A/77987.

Department of the Environment, 1970. *Brent Cross, Barnet, London*. File No. P1/4404/219/7B.

Department of the Environment, 1972a. *Wolvercote, Oxford*. File No. PF3/2307A/2201.

Department of the Environment, 1972b. *Chandlers Ford, Eastleigh, Hants*. File Nos. APP/1070/A/50692, 55375.

Department of the Environment, 1972c. *Out of town shops and shopping centres*. Development Control Policy Note No. 13, H.M.S.O., London.

Department of the Environment, 1972d. *Asda, Great Yarmouth.*
File No. PD3/1153/219/23.

Department of the Environment, 1973a. *Carrefour, Shenstone,
Lichfield.* File No. PE1/2193/219/23.

Department of the Environment, 1973b. *Woolco, Twyford,
Berks.* File No. PF3/2522/219/23.

Department of the Environment, 1974. *Cribbs Causeway.*
File Nos. PD2/2424/220/2, PD2/2424/220/3,
PD2/2424/220/10, PD2/2424/220/11, PD2/2424/220/12.

Department of the Environment, 1975a. *Stonebridge, Solihull.*
File No. WMR/P/2243/182/1.

Department of the Environment, 1975b. *Roselands, Broxtowe,
Nottinghamshire.* File No. APP/835/A/63253.

Department of the Environment, 1975c. *Supa K, North Benfleet,
Essex.* File No. APP/1539A/A/72085.

Department of the Environment, 1975d. *Carrefour, Rawreth,
Essex.* File No. APP/1539A/A/73466.

Department of the Environment, 1975e. *Carrefour, Minworth,
Birmingham.* File No. WMR/P/5104/220/2.

Department of the Environment, 1975f. *R.A.C.S., St. Peter's,
Thanet.* File Nos. APP/906/A/67580, APP/5283/A/74/6758.

Department of the Environment, 1976a. *The Eastleigh
Carrefour: a hypermarket and its effects.* Research
Report No. 16, (Department of the Environment, London).

Department of the Environment, 1976b. *Large new stores.*
Joint Circular of the Department of the Environment
and the Welsh Office, Circulars 71/76; 98/76, (London
and Cardiff).

Department of the Environment, 1977a. *Large new stores.*
Revisions to Development Control Policy Note No. 13,
1972, (H.M.S.O., London).

Department of the Environment, 1977b. *Colchester Superstore
and hypermarket proposals.* File Nos. APP/5214/A/75/994,
EI/5214/42/5, APP/5214/A/76/4259.

Department of the Environment, 1978. *The Eastleigh
Carrefour hypermarket after three years.* Research
Report No. 27, (Department of the Environment, London).

Department of the Environment, 1981a. *Coventry SavaCentre.*
File No. APP/5399/A/79/3643.

Department of the Environment, 1981b. *Croydon hypermarket.*
File No. APP/5009/A/80/10447.

Department of the Environment, 1982a. *Rochdale D.I.Y.
centre.* File No. T/APP/5084/A81/11648/G6.

Department of the Environment, 1982b. *Sainsbury's
superstore, Exeter.* File No. T/APP/5177/A/82/831/G4.

Department of Industry, 1975. *Report on the census of
distribution and other services, 1971.* (H.M.S.O.,
London).

Department of Industry, 1980. *Business monitor: retailing.* Business Statistics Office, SDA 25, (H.M.S.O., London).

Department of Trade and Industry, 1971. *Report on the census of distribution and other services, 1966.* (H.M.S.O., London).

Department of Trade and Industry, 1973. *Report on the census of England and Wales, 1971: the availability of cars.* (H.M.S.O., London).

Gayler, H.J. 1979. *The out-of-town shopping centre in the United Kingdom: some aspects of resistance to retail change.* Paper presented to the Association of American Geographers Conference, Philadelphia, April 1979.

Gibbs, A. 1981. *An analysis of retail warehouse planning inquiries.* Report U22, (The Unit for Retail Planning Information, Reading).

Gibbs, A. 1982. *Retail warehouses.* Unpublished discussion paper, Department of Geography, University of Reading, Reading.

Gilham, K. 1976. Hypermarkets - a necessary evil? *The Architect's Journal,* 163(18), 881-910.

Gloucestershire C.C., Gloucester B.C. and Cheltenham B.C. 1970. *North Gloucestershire sub-regional study.* Gloucestershire C.C., Gloucester).

Guy, C.M. 1976. *The location of shops in the Reading area.* Geographical Paper No. 46, (Department of Geography, University of Reading, Reading).

Guy, C.M. 1980. *Retail location and retail planning in Britain.* (Gower, Farnborough).

Hall, P. 1974. *Urban and regional planning.* (Penguin, Harmondsworth).

Hall, P., Gracey, H., Drewett, R. and Thomas, R. 1973. *The containment of urban England.* 2 vols. (Allen and Unwin, London).

Hillman, M. 1973. The social costs of hypermarket development. *Built Environment,* 2, 89-91.

Hillman, M., Henderson, I. and Whalley, A. 1972. In the market place: the hypermarket debate. *New Society,* 21(520), 543-546.

I.P.C. Women's Weekly Group, 1970. *Shopping in the seventies.* (I.P.C., London).

I.P.C. Women's Weekly Group, 1975. *Food, clothing, drink and tobacco.* (I.P.C., London).

Institute of Food Distribution, 1970. *Directory 1970.* (Institute of Food Distribution, London).

Institute of Grocery Distribution, 1982. *Superstores Directory 1982.* (Institute of Grocery Distribution, Watford).

Jackson, J.N. 1972. *The urban future.* (Allen and Unwin, London).

Jones, C.S. 1969. *Regional shopping centres: their location, planning and design.* (Business Books, London).

Jones, P. 1981. Retail innovation and diffusion: the spread of Asda stores. *Area,* 13, 197-201.

Jones, P. 1982a. Retail warehouses. *Geography,* 67, 139-141.

Jones, P. 1982b. The locational policies and geographical expansion of multiple retail companies: a case study of M.F.I. *Geoforum,* 13, 39-43.

Jones, P.M. 1978. *Trading features of hypermarkets and superstores.* Report U7, (The Unit for Retail Planning Information, Reading).

Jones, P.M. 1982. Hypermarkets and superstores: future growth or saturation? *Estates Gazette,* 262, 843-847.

Kivell, P.T. 1972. Retailing in non-central locations. *Institute of British Geographers,* Occasional Publication No. 1, 49-58.

Lee, M., Jones, P. and Leach, C. 1973. *Caerphilly hypermarket study.* (Donaldsons, London).

Lee, M. and Kent, E. 1975. *Caerphilly hypermarket study year two.* (Donaldsons, London).

Lee, M. and Kent, E. 1976. *Planning inquiry study.* (Donaldsons, London).

Lee, M. and Kent, E. 1977. *Brent Cross study.* (Donaldsons, London).

Lee, M. and Kent, E. 1978. *Planning inquiry study two.* (Donaldsons, London).

Lee, M. and Kent, E. 1979. *Caerphilly hypermarket study year five.* (Donaldsons, London).

Lee, M. and Roberts, C. 1981. *Planning inquiry study three.* (Donaldsons, London).

Mansley, R.D. and Verrico, R. 1971. *Shopping centres and hypermarket developments in and around Glasgow.* (Corporation Planning Dept., Glasgow).

Mills, E. 1974. *Recent developments in retailing and urban planning.* P.R.A.G. Technical Papers TP3, (Planning Research Applications Group, London).

Ministry of Housing and Local Government, 1969. *The development of district shopping centres in towns with central area traffic congestion.* (Ministry of Housing and Local Government, London).

Moir, C.B. 1981. Retailing in the inner city area. *P.I.R.C.,* Summer Meeting, 9-18.

National Economic Development Office, 1968. *The Cowley shopping centre.* (H.M.S.O., London).

National Economic Development Office, 1970. *Urban models in shopping studies*. (N.E.D.O., London).

National Economic Development Office, 1971. *The future pattern of shopping*. (H.M.S.O., London).

National Economic Development Office, 1981. *Retailing in inner cities*. (H.M.S.O., London).

Neilsen, A.C. & Co., 1977. *Grocery superstores*. Neilsen Researcher No. 2, (A.C. Neilsen & Co., London).

Newby, P.T. and Shepherd, I.D.H. 1979. Brent Cross: a milestone in retail development. *Geography*, 64, 133-137.

Nottinghamshire-Derbyshire Sub-Regional Planning Unit, 1969. *Nottinghamshire and Derbyshire sub-regional study*. (Alfreton).

Pacione, M. 1979. The in-town hypermarket: an innovation in the geography of retailing. *Regional Studies*, 13, 15-24.

Pain, G.M. 1967. *Planning and the shopkeeper*. (Barrie and Rockliff, London).

Pollard, D.S. and Hughes, J.D. 1955. Retailing costs. *Oxford Economic Papers*, 7, 71-93.

Ridgway, J.D. 1981. Modern retailing as a spur to urban regeneration. *P.I.R.C.*, Summer Meeting, 19-28.

Rogers, D.S. 1974. *Bretton, Peterborough: the impact of a large edge-of-town supermarket*. Research Report No. 9, (Manchester Business School Retail Outlets Research Unit, Manchester).

Rogers, D.S. 1979. Evaluating the business and planning impacts of suburban shopping developments: a proposed framework of analysis. *Regional Studies*, 13, 395-408.

Scott, P. 1970. *Geography and Retailing*. (Hutchinson, London).

Shepherd, I. and Newby, P. 1978. *The Brent Cross regional shopping centre: characteristics and early effects*. (Retailing and Planning Associates, Corbridge, Northumberland).

Smith, B.A. 1973. Retail planning in France: the changing pattern of French retailing. *Town Planning Review*, 44, 279-306.

Smith, R.D. 1968. The changing urban hierarchy. *Regional Studies*, 2, 1-19.

Solesbury, W. 1975. Ideas about Structure Plans: past, present and future. *Town Planning Review*, 46, 245-254.

South Hampshire Plan Advisory Committee, 1972a. *South Hampshire Structure Plan: report of the survey*. (Hampshire C.C., Portsmouth C.B.C. and Southampton C.B.C., Winchester).

South Hampshire Plan Advisory Committee, 1972b. *South Hampshire Structure Plan: draft document for participation and consultation*. (Hampshire C.C., Portsmouth C.B.C. and Southampton C.B.C., Winchester).

Sternlieb, G. and Hughes, J.W. (eds.) 1981. *Shopping centres: U.S.A.* (Rutgers University Center for Urban Policy Research, Piscataway, N.J.).

Sunderland Corporation, 1971. *The Sunderland hypermarket survey*. (Sunderland Corporation, Sunderland).

Taylor, P.J. 1972. Letter to the editor. *New Society*, 22(523), 107.

Thomas, C.J., Thorpe, D. and McGoldrick P.J. 1977. *Co-operative Society superstores*. Research Report No. 22, (Manchester Business School Retail Outlets Research Unit, Manchester).

Thomas, D. 1970. *London's green belt*. (Faber and Faber, London).

Thorncroft, M. 1973. British superstores. *Built Environment*, 2, 94-97.

Thorpe, D. 1968. The main shopping centres of Great Britain in 1961: their locational and structural characteristics. *Urban Studies*, 5, 165-206.

Thorpe, D. 1978a. *Shopping trip patterns and the spread of superstores and hypermarkets in Great Britain*. Research Paper No. 10, (Manchester Business School Retail Outlets Research Unit, Manchester).

Thorpe, D. 1978b. Progress in the study of the geography of retail and wholesaling in Britain. *Geoforum*, 9, 83-106.

Thorpe, D., Bates, P. and Shepherd, P. 1977. *Retail structure town planning: superstore impact and long term trends*. (Planning and Transportation Research, London).

Thorpe, D. and Kivell, P.T. 1971. *Woolco Thornaby: a study of an out-of-town shopping centre*. (Manchester Business School Retail Outlets Research Unit, Manchester).

Thorpe, D., Kivell, P.T., Pratley, R. and Andrews, M. 1972. *The Hampshire Centre, Bournemouth: a study of an out-of-town shopping centre*. (Manchester Business School Retail Outlets Research Unit, Manchester).

Thorpe, D. and McGoldrick, P.J. 1974a. *Superstores, discounters and a covered centre: a study of competition in North Manchester*. Research Report No. 11, (Manchester Business School Retail Outlets Research Unit, Manchester).

Thorpe, D. and McGoldrick, P.J. 1974b. *Carrefour: Caerphilly consumer reaction*. Research Report No. 12, (Manchester Business School Retail Outlets Research Unit, Manchester).

Thorpe, D. and McGoldrick, P.J. 1977. Co-op Failsworth. in: Thomas, C.J., Thorpe, D. and McGoldrick, P.J. (eds.), *Co-operative Society superstores*. Research Report No. 22, (Manchester Business School Retail Outlets Research Unit, Manchester).

Thorpe, D. and Nader, G.A. 1967. Customer movement and shopping centre structure. *Regional Studies*, 1, 173-191.

Unit for Retail Planning Information, 1976. *Hypermarkets and superstores: report of a House of Commons seminar, May 1976*. (The Unit for Retail Planning Information, Reading).

Unit for Retail Planning Information, 1982. *List of U.K. hypermarkets and superstores 8th edition*. (The Unit for Retail Planning Information, Reading).

University of Manchester Department of Town and Country Planning, 1964. *Regional shopping centres in North West England*. (Manchester).

Index

Roselands (Broxstowe, Notts.), 20
Rural-urban conflict (see Urban encroachment)

Sainsbury's, 73, 74, 75, 77, 79, 94, 103-104, 121
SavaCentres, 69, 117-118, 120
Social class appeal, 45-47
South Hampshire Structure Plan, 29, 99
Stonebridge (Solihull), 20
Structure plans, 29, 57, 60, 74, 76, 89, 91-92, 93,
     100-105, 112-113, 126, 128
Sub-regional planning, 91, 98-99, 100
Suburbanisation, 3, 10-11, 54
Supermarkets, development of, 14-18, 24, 114, 123
Superstores
   appeal, 46, 49-51, 124
   design, 64-66
   development of, 16-18, 19, 114, 123
   impact of, 24 -25, 30-31, 37-43, 116-117, 129
   site characteristics, 62-66
   trade areas, 36-39

Tesco stores, 41, 42, 43, 83, 117
Town centres, 14, 27, 28, 30, 51, 64, 69, 71, 81-85, 88,
     90-92, 95, 99, 100, 107, 113, 118, 126, 130
Traffic hazards, 60-62, 120-121

Unit for Retail Planning Information, 16, 89
Urban encroachment, 54-58, 60, 70, 75, 124-125
Urban renewal, 10

West End (Central London), 19, 68
Weston Favell (Northampton), 18, 25
Western European shopping centres, 2, 16-17, 18, 50-51
Wolvercote (Oxford), 20, 68
Woolco stores, 19, 37, 60, 62